"This important book reminds _____ g ___ ___ ___ ____ ____ that
liturgy is primarily not about what we do for God but what
God does for us in a unique way through the liturgy.
Throughout Boselli penetrates to the spiritual heart of the
liturgy. A much-needed book at a time when debates about
liturgy are all too often about externals, not the inner depth of
what liturgy is and does. The author's invitation that we truly
'listen' to God speaking to us through word and sacrament—as
simple as that sounds—is a much-needed lesson not only
about liturgy but about the Christian life."

> —Rev Msgr. Kevin W. Irwin
> The Catholic University of America

"In this book, we come to understand better the connections
between what we do in the liturgy and our spiritual
relationship with Christ. Contemplation and interiority arise
from ritual action and communal experience: this is the
paradox that makes this volume a precious occasion for
personal and communal reflection on the topic."

> —Andrea Grillo
> Professor of Sacramental Theology
> Pontifical Atheneum of Saint Anselm, Rome
> Author of *Beyond Pius V: Conflicting
>     Interpretations of the Liturgical Reform*

"This book offers a sound mystagogy based primarily on
Scripture and the writings of the fathers that will be of value
to those engaged in the task of liturgical formation."

> —Paul F. Bradshaw
> Professor of Liturgy (Emeritus)
> University of Notre Dame
> Author of *Rites of Ordination: Their History
>     and Theology*

"Reading Boselli's book is like going on retreat. He has meditated deeply on links between liturgical actions and the words of Scripture. You will enter a profound reflection on the Eucharist you share and the life you lead."

—Paul Turner, Pastor, St. Anthony Parish,
Kansas City, Missouri
Facilitator, International Commission on
English in the Liturgy

"Today perhaps more than ever we need to deepen our spiritual understanding of the church's liturgy. Boselli provides us with a genuine mystagogy, leading to a profound appreciation of the depths of the liturgy and rooted solidly in the Scriptures and the early Christian writers. His work brings out the nature of the liturgy as primarily a gift from God, God's work among us, calling us to listen to his word and respond. It will be of enormous value to ministers, scholars, and the worshiping faithful alike."

—John F. Baldovin, SJ
Professor of Historical and Liturgical Theology
Boston College School of Theology and Ministry

# The Spiritual Meaning of the Liturgy

*School of Prayer, Source of Life*

Goffredo Boselli

Translated by Barry Hudock

Foreword by Paul De Clerck

LITURGICAL PRESS

Collegeville, Minnesota

www.litpress.org

Cover design by Jodi Hendrickson. Illustration: *The Liturgical Path of the Christian*, miniature (eleventh century), Commentary on the Canticle of Canticles, ms. Bibl. 22, f. 4v, Staatsbibliothek, Bamberg.

Excerpts from the English translation of the General Instruction from *The Liturgy of the Hours* © 1973, 1974, 1975, International Commission on English in the Liturgy Corporation (ICEL); excerpts from the English translation of *Eucharistic Prayers for Masses with Children* © 1975, ICEL; excerpts from the English translation of *The Roman Missal* © 2010, ICEL. All rights reserved.

Unless otherwise indicated, excerpts from documents of the Second Vatican Council are from *Vatican Council II: The Basic Sixteen Documents*, edited by Austin Flannery, OP, © 1996. Used with permission of Liturgical Press, Collegeville, Minnesota.

Unless otherwise indicated, Scripture texts in this work are taken from the *New Revised Standard Version Bible* © 1989, Division of Christian Education of the National Council of the Churches of Christ in the United States of America. Used by permission. All rights reserved.

1    2    3    4    5    6    7    8    9

**Library of Congress Cataloging-in-Publication Data**

Boselli, Goffredo.
    [Senso spirituale della liturgia. English]
    The spiritual meaning of the liturgy : school of prayer, source of life / Goffredo Boselli ; translated by Barry Hudock ; foreword by Paul De Clerck.
        pages   cm
    "A Liturgical Press book."
    ISBN 978-0-8146-4906-0 — ISBN 978-0-8146-4919-0 (ebook)
    1. Catholic Church—Liturgy—History—20th century.  2. Catholic Church—Liturgy—History—21st century.  3. Liturgics.  I. Title.
BX1975.B6713   2014
264'.02—dc23                              2014011979

# Contents

Foreword   vii
  *Paul De Clerck*

Translator's Note   x

Introduction   xi

Part One: Mystagogy

  Chapter 1: Introduction to Mystagogy   3

  Chapter 2: Mystagogy of the Penitential Act   23

  Chapter 3: Mystagogy of the Liturgy
            of the Word   47

  Chapter 4: Mystagogy of the Presentation
            of the Gifts   79

Part Two: Liturgy in the Life of the Church

  Chapter 5: The Sacrament of the Assembly   105

  Chapter 6: Presbyters Formed by the Liturgy   131

  Chapter 7: The Missal, Book of the Prayer
            of the Church   145

  Chapter 8: The Liturgy, School of Prayer   161

Part Three:  A Liturgy for the Christianity
              That Lies Ahead of Us

    Chapter 9:   Liturgy and Love for the Poor   183

    Chapter 10:  Liturgy and the Transmission
                of the Faith   209

Conclusion:  The Liturgy Is the Most Efficacious Action
             of the Church   231

# Foreword

You have in your hands an important book. It sheds light on the current situation of the liturgy, fifty years after the Second Vatican Council and initial efforts at applying the Constitution *Sacrosanctum Concilium*. This distance in time allows the author to take account of the long experience of the liturgical reform, including a deeper understanding of the very meaning of the liturgy itself. In fact, it is in regard to the latter topic that this book makes its most significant contributions. In a certain sense, the introduction summarizes well everything the book has to say:

> [T]he future of Christianity in the West depends largely on the church's capacity to allow its liturgy to become the source of the spiritual life of all believers. For this reason, the liturgy represents an important challenge for the church today. I am increasingly convinced that the decisive question that demands an answer from us is not so much how believers experience the liturgy but whether believers live from the liturgy they celebrate.

So that Christians can live from the liturgy, Goffredo Boselli offers us a method: mystagogy. Just as *lectio divina* allows us to penetrate the depths of the meaning of the Scriptures and to live that meaning more authentically, mystagogy introduces us to the mystery. "What *lectio divina* is for Scripture, mystagogy is for the liturgy." Unlike

those who conceive understanding the liturgy as intellec-
tually subduing and making its contents our own, here we
read that "in celebrating the mystery, we are initiated into
the mystery." "[The] close connection between Scripture
and liturgy is the essence of the fathers' spiritual intuition,
and it is made concrete through mystagogy."

The author presents his thinking over a series of chapters, offering a mystagogy of several key moments of the
eucharistic liturgy and exploring topics such as the role of
the liturgy in the life of the church, liturgy and love for the
poor, and the way the liturgy transmits the faith. The author, though a monk, is not satisfied to confine his thoughts
to matters of spirituality. He is attentive at all times to the
liturgical-theological foundation of his thinking, taking,
for example, the ritual of the breaking of the bread as a
starting point for identifying the social consequences of
the celebration. He is able constantly to extract from the
rites their quintessence, in the sure conviction that the
meaning of the liturgy must determine liturgical praxis,
and for this reason the first and fundamental school of the
liturgy is the liturgy itself. Each of these chapters are
marked profoundly by a living awareness that the liturgy
provides its own explanation of itself, naturally, and that
it bears great theological importance for Christians of
today and tomorrow. Throughout the presentation of his
arguments, the author demonstrates his thorough immer-
sion in a solid biblical and patristic, theological and liturgical culture.

In his final chapter, on the relationship between the liturgy and the transmission of the faith, a certain disquiet
emerges. I perceive in those pages a tension, if not even
an opposition between an authentically spiritual liturgy
and the convivial character with which many today wish
to imbue the celebration. Is there necessarily opposition

between these two goals? Is there not a way to reconcile them, giving a distinctive a rhythm to the celebration?

Throughout this work, Goffredo Boselli demonstrates himself to be a man grounded in mystery. He has integrated the profound meaning of the liturgy, living it personally and communicating it in a style that is both intelligent and accessible. We might say that this book marks the beginning of a second stage of the postconciliar liturgical reform: following the publication of the new rites and their initial reception, it is time for a theological deepening; this is very necessary today and it is coming about. It is a step forward in our understanding of the liturgy!

> Paul De Clerck
> Professor
> Institut supérieur de liturgie
> Institut catholique de Paris

# Translator's Note

I have made strong efforts to provide patristic translations from the appropriate English sources. Where the available translations are dated, I have occasionally made some minor revisions to eliminate obvious English archaisms. In some cases, where published patristic translations were not available to me, I translated passages directly from Br. Boselli's Italian text. I have noted the instances where this has occurred.

# Introduction

*"We . . . worship in the Spirit of God."*
—Philippians 3:3

One often gets the impression today that the liturgy is perceived more as a problem to be solved than as a source of life. And yet the future of Christianity in the West depends largely on the church's capacity to allow its liturgy to become the source of spiritual life of all believers. For this reason, the liturgy represents an important challenge for the church today. I am increasingly convinced that the decisive question that demands an answer from us is not so much how believers experience the liturgy but whether believers *live from the liturgy* they celebrate. How believers experience the liturgy, in fact, depends on how they live from the liturgy. To live from the liturgy one celebrates means to live from what one experiences there: mercy invoked, the word of God heard, thanks given, Eucharist received as communion. If believers live from the liturgy, they will experience it differently, because it bears within it the spiritual energies that are essential for their growth in the spiritual life. The liturgy, in fact, is the specific way the church lives from Christ and through Christ and enables believers to live from Christ and through Christ. The liturgical words and gestures are ordered to this: "[T]o me, living is Christ" (Phil 1:21).

It is not at all obvious that the liturgy might be a spiritual experience, because one can celebrate liturgy throughout one's life without ever drawing one's life from it. And this is true of all believers without distinction: laity, clergy, or monastics. More than a century after the start of the liturgical movement and half a century after the start of the postconciliar liturgical reform, we must ask the difficult question of whether the liturgy has or has not become the source of the spiritual life of believers.

The great Christian tradition has always considered the liturgy to be the fertile womb of the church from which Christians are born. The liturgy is parturient. It gives life. For this reason the liturgy does not choose its own purpose but receives it from the holy reality that it celebrates and which it serves exclusively: the mystery of God in Christ, which we confess in the Creed to be "[f]or us men and for our salvation."[1] Like the mystery that it celebrates, the liturgy, too, is for us and for our salvation. For this reason, the purpose of the liturgy is the sanctification of people; it is through holiness of life that one gives glory to God. Therefore, the decisive criterion on which one can judge the quality of the liturgy can be nothing other than the quality of the spiritual lives of those who celebrate it. It is necessary, then, to put before all other liturgical concerns the goal that Christians find in the liturgy the nourishment of their lives of faith, that they never celebrate the liturgy without living from it.

We must recognize that while believers have been taught, in recent decades, how to draw nourishment for their spiritual lives from the Scriptures, they have not been taught to draw it in a similar way from the liturgy. Half a century after

---

1. *The Roman Missal, Third Edition* (Collegeville, MN: Liturgical Press, 2011), 527.

the important choice of the council to draw the word of God closer to the heart of the church, we have seen remarkable growth in awareness of the Bible by Christians, thanks in part to the rediscovery of *lectio divina*, brought about by monastics and pastors who have carefully broken and shared the bread of the Word. We have seen the spontaneous growth of a great number of Bible study groups where the laity meet weekly to read and meditate together on the Sunday readings or on entire books of Scripture. Many observers suggest that in the history of the church there has never been such a great awareness of the Bible by the people of God as there is today. Can we say the same of the liturgy?

Despite the profound renewal brought about by the conciliar liturgical reform and the undeniable benefits that have come with the reestablishment of the connection of the liturgy to believers and believers to the liturgy, it is still not possible to say that the liturgy is the nourishment of the spiritual life of believers in the same way that can be said today of the Scriptures. In reality, what happened in regard to the Bible has not happened in regard to the liturgy. By introducing believers to *lectio divina*, we have taught them a method for knowing and understanding the Bible, an interpretive key so that every single Christian can personally approach the word of God contained in the Scriptures. We placed in the hands of believers not only the Bible but also a tool that has enabled them to draw from the Scriptures the necessary food for their lives of faith. Although there is still a long way to go, the reconnection of believers to the Scriptures is today a reality that would have been unthinkable only fifty years ago. When the conditions were provided that made it possible for believers to understand, because they were taught a suitable and effective method for approaching a task as complex and demanding as hearing the word of God contained in the Scriptures, it became possible.

In the same way, the church could provide the conditions that enable believers to live from the liturgy by teaching them a method for understanding the liturgy they celebrate. It is urgent to teach a sort of *lectio* of the liturgy that helps Christians understand the meaning of the liturgical texts and gestures in order to interiorize the mystery they celebrate. This would mean, for example, approaching the mystery of the Eucharist by understanding the meaning of the eucharistic prayer. To interiorize the dynamic and the content of the anaphora would mean nourishing one's life of faith with the church's eucharistic faith in its highest and fullest expression. As long as believers draw their understanding of the Eucharist from other places, they will be unable fully to live from the mystery of the Eucharist as it is celebrated by the church. It may well be an authentic eucharistic faith, but it will also be an incomplete one. An illuminating example in this regard was offered by the bishops of France in 1978, when they published a small catechism called *Il est grande le mystère de la foi*, which presented all of the essential points of Christian faith by taking as its starting point Eucharistic Prayer IV. In the introduction to their catechism, the bishops wrote:

> The church believes as it prays. Every eucharistic celebration is a profession of faith. The rule of prayer is the rule of faith. For this reason, we French bishops, wishing to present to Catholics in our dioceses the essential aspects of the mystery of faith, offer not a new document but a text already known to many: the eucharistic prayer. . . . We believe all that the church of Christ believes, all that is expressed in the eucharistic prayer.[2]

2. The Bishops of France, *Il est grande le mystère de la foi. Prière et foi de l'Église catholique* (Paris: Éditions du Centurion, 1978), 3.

The adage *lex orandi, lex credendi* is valid not only for the church as a whole but as a principle of every single Christian's life of faith. If the church believes as it prays, so every Christian is called to believe as he or she prays with the church.

For believers to live from the liturgy, they must have a method that allows them to draw directly from the source of the church's prayer. Like the holy Scripture, the liturgy must be understood, meditated upon, and interiorized until it becomes a part of personal prayer. I am referring not merely to intellectual understanding but to a spiritual and existential understanding that certainly includes an intellectual aspect. The question posed by the apostle Philip in the Acts of the Apostles to the Ethiopian official whom he finds reading the prophet Isaiah—"Do you understand what you are reading?" (Acts 8:30)—should also be asked regarding the liturgy: "Do you understand what you are celebrating?" The response of the Christian people is the same as that offered by the Ethiopian: "How can I, unless someone guides me?" (Acts 8:31). To guide into the mystery is, in Greek, *mystagoghêin*. Mystagogy is a method and a tool that the ancient church offers us to help the faithful live what they celebrate. What *lectio divina* is for Scripture, mystagogy is for the liturgy. The great fruits borne in recent years by the practice of *lectio divina* among the Christian faithful teach us that there is no place for resignation or cynicism in these efforts. The ongoing success of *lectio divina* has demonstrated that it is possible to teach Christians to drink from the pure source of their faith. This has been happening now for several decades with regard to Scripture, while with the liturgy it is largely yet to be realized.

This book is a little contribution that seeks to move us in this direction. It is a collection of texts that I have written in recent years for various occasions and circumstances. Essentially a collection, it does not have the linear

and uniform structure that one might expect of a mono-
graph. Put in musical terms, we might say that it does not
have the ordered and established unity of a symphony but
the irregular pace of a rhapsody in which different themes
freely intermingle. But the golden thread that runs through
it and in a certain way gives it form is the need for a spiritual reading of the liturgy.

Part 1 is about mystagogy, its meaning and its use. I
propose a mystagogical reading of several parts of the eucharistic liturgy—the penitential act, the Liturgy of the
Word, and the presentation of the gifts—showing that the
liturgy takes not only its meaning but also its structure and
its dynamic from Scripture. Part 2 considers the role of
the liturgy in the life of the church, and through various
themes—assembly, presbyter, missal, prayer—I seek to
show that the way the church prays establishes not only
what the church believes but what the church *is*, to the
point that the liturgy challenges our way of being church.
Part 3 explores the Eucharist as the source of social ethics
and the role of the liturgy in the transmission of the faith.
Here I seek to show the relevance of the liturgy to the
church's *hodie*—the circumstances and situations of
today—which is always at the same time the *hodie* of society and of the world.

Bose
April 21, 2011
Holy Thursday

# Part One
# Mystagogy

# Chapter One

# Introduction to Mystagogy

*[H]e who is still blind and dumb, not having under-
standing . . . like the uninitiated at the mysteries, or
the unmusical at dances . . . must stand outside of
the divine choir.*

—Clement of Alexandria[1]

## *The Liturgy Initiates Us into the Mystery*

Mystagogy is bound up with the reality of the mystery of
God. It is ordered to that mystery of which the liturgy is an
epiphany.[2] To speak of mystagogy immediately calls to mind
the catecheses and homilies with which some of the most
important fathers of the church—including Cyril (or John)
of Jerusalem, Ambrose of Milan, John Chrysostom, Theodore of Mopsuestia—introduced their catechumens and
neophytes to the meaning of baptism, Eucharist, and more

1. Clement of Alexandria, *The Stromata*, 5.4, in *The Ante-Nicene Fathers*, vol. 2, ed. Alexander Roberts, James Donaldson, and A. Cleveland Coxe, trans. William Wilson (Buffalo: Christian Literature Publishing Co., 1885), 449.
2. This chapter was originally published as "La mistagogia per entrare nel mistero," in Enzo Bianchi and Goffredo Boselli, *La liturgia, epifania del mistero* (Bose: Qiqajon, 2002).

generally, the major elements of Christian liturgy. But there is more to mystagogy than the mystagogical catecheses of the fathers. It is, in fact, a vast, many-faceted, and extremely complex reality that cannot be limited solely to liturgical initiation.

The scholar René Bornert effectively summarized all the complexity of mystagogy in two principle definitions. Mystagogy "is in the first place the accomplishment of a sacred action and in particular the celebration of the sacraments of initiation, baptism, and Eucharist."[3] To say that mystagogy is first of all a liturgical action means the liturgy is, in itself, mystagogy. It is by its nature an epiphany of the mystery of God; in celebrating the mystery, we are initiated into the mystery. For the fathers of the church, then, the celebration of the mysteries is already initiation into the mysteries. Through liturgy, the mystery is revealed, communicated, made known. This is to say that liturgy is a theological act, an action of God, and for this reason, it accomplishes what it signifies. As is well known, Benedict, in his Rule, never uses the word *liturgy* to refer to this reality but always the expression *opus Dei,* the work of God. To describe the liturgy as *opus Dei* is to attribute to God's action in the liturgy the same qualities that Scripture recognizes as belonging to the word of God, a word that is, in itself, act, a word that accomplishes what it signifies. Through the prophet Isaiah, God describes the nature of the word that comes from his mouth:

> it shall not return to me empty,
> but it shall accomplish that which I purpose,
> and succeed in the thing for which I sent it. (Isa 55:11)

3. René Bornert, *Les commentaires byzantins de la Divine liturgie du VII<sup>e</sup> au XV<sup>e</sup> siècle* (Paris: Institut français d'etudes byzantines, 1966), 29.

Bornert offers a second meaning of mystagogy: it is "the oral or written explanation of the mystery that is hidden in the Scripture and celebrated in the liturgy."[4] Mystagogy takes account of both the mystery contained in the Scriptures and the mystery contained in the liturgy. The object is one: the mystery of God. The modalities of expression of the mystery are two: Scripture and liturgy. And the method of explanation for both is the same: mystagogy. The great spiritual intuition that the fathers expressed in their mystagogical catecheses was to apply the same method they used to interpret Scripture to their interpretation of the liturgy. Using the same method of interpretation, the same hermeneutic for two distinct realities, means recognizing in these two realities a profound and essential unity, while never denying their distinction, their difference, and the preeminence of the Scriptures over the liturgy. Indeed, the Scriptures are the norm of the liturgy. This close connection between Scriptures and liturgy is the essence of the fathers' spiritual intuition, and it is made concrete through mystagogy. It is also the reason for mystagogy's profound relevance for the church of our own day.

## Jesus Christ, Mystagogue

To begin by understanding mystagogy as an eminently christological action means above all to affirm that only the mystery can fully reveal the mystery: mystery reveals itself. This is an essential truth of the Judeo-Christian faith experience: humanity knows God's name because God has freely revealed it. The revelation of the mystery of God is an act that God carries out.

4. Ibid.

In Jewish apocalyptic literature—in which the Christian understanding of mystery is deeply rooted—the mystery (*mystérion* in the Greek Bible) is the secret, divine plan that God alone can reveal to his servants the prophets, as Amos proclaimed:

> Surely the Lord GOD does nothing,
> without revealing his secret
> to his servants the prophets. (Amos 3:7)

To the prophet Daniel "the mystery was revealed . . . in a vision of the night" (Dan 2:19), and when the king of Babylon, Nebuchadnezzar, orders him to explain the mystery contained in his dream, Daniel responds, "No wise men, enchanters, magicians, or diviners can show to the king the mystery that the king is asking, but there is a God in heaven who reveals mysteries" (Dan 2:27-28). To reveal the mystery is the work of God alone.

Like the prophet Daniel, the apostle Paul sees himself as one who comes "proclaiming the mystery of God" (1 Cor 2:1). He asserts that "the mystery was made known to me by revelation" (Eph 3:3). And for Paul, the mystery is God's plan "to gather up all things in [Christ]" (Eph 1:10), and so that mystery is, in sum, Christ himself, revealed fully in his death on the cross. Christ is, for Paul, not only the revealer of the mystery but is himself the mystery of God. In the synoptics, too, in the only place the word *mystery* occurs, we find the idea that God alone is the revealer of the mystery. It is Jesus himself who, in the context of explaining to his disciples the parables of the Kingdom, says, "[K]nowledge of the mysteries of the kingdom of heaven has been granted to you, but to them it has not been granted" (Matt 13:11 NABRE; cf. Mark 4:10; Luke 8:10). Therefore, the one who entrusts to his disciples "the mystery of the kingdom" is Jesus, "the prophet mighty in deed and word" (Luke 24:19).

Despite this profound understanding of Christ as revealer of the mystery of God, the term *mystagogy* appears nowhere in Paul or anywhere else in the New Testament to designate initiation into the mystery, nor is the title of *mystagogue* attributed to Jesus. This can be explained by the fact that in the Jewish tradition it was the *rabbi* whose role it was to introduce his disciples to the knowledge of God, above all through commentary on the Scriptures.

But in the third and fourth centuries, in places rich in Greek culture like Alexandria and the churches of Asia Minor, Christian authors like Origen and fathers of the church Clement of Alexandria, Gregory of Nazianzus, Gregory of Nyssa, John Chrysostom, and others take a decisive step. The fathers did not assume the Greek concept of mystery, since for the Greeks mystery was a reality that had to remain hidden and of which one could not speak. The Greek understanding of mystery, then, is exactly the opposite of the Judeo-Christian one, for which the mystery is the revelation of the secret of God and God's will. The fathers of the church limit themselves to recognizing in the Greek term *mystagoghía* its sense of initiation into the cultic mysteries by the mystagogue, a term adequate for describing much of Jesus' teaching of the disciples and the crowds, as well as the preaching of the Gospel by the apostles. The preaching of Paul is described as mystagogy by, among others, Gregory of Nyssa: "Paul . . . initiates the people of Ephesus in the mysteries (*mystagoghei*) and imbues them through his instructions with the power of knowing what is that 'depth and height and breadth and length' [of the knowledge of God]."[5] At

5. Gregory of Nyssa, Catechetical Discourse 32, in *Gregory of Nyssa: Select Writings and Letters*, Nicene and Post-Nicene Fathers of the Christian Church, vol. 5, ed. Philip Schaff and Henry Wace (Grand Rapids, MI: Eerdmans, 1956), 500.

Antioch, John Chrysostom preaches, "Paul is to be seen in prison, even in chains, instructing and initiating [*mystagoûnta*: offering mystagogy], even in a court of justice, in shipwreck, in a storm, and in a thousand dangers."[6]

On Jesus as mystagogue, it is enough to mention two witnesses. Gregory of Nazianzus, who in *Christus patiens*—a work that is a true and proper tragedy in the style of the Greek tragedies—puts in the mouth of an anonymous person this cry addressed to Judas: "You are the initiated into the mystery (*mýstes*) and you dishonor your fellow disciples by handing over for money your mystagogue (*mystagogón*)."[7] For Gregory, then, Jesus is the mystagogue of his disciples, and the twelve then become the initiated who in turn initiate others to the mystery of God. In the same way, Cyril of Alexandria, in his *Commentary on the Gospel of Luke*, says regarding the episode of Jesus teaching the crowd at Capernaum and the healing of the demoniac that immediately follows, "It was useful and necessary that Christ often followed his mystagogy with miracles."[8] It is clear, then, that Cyril does not hesitate then to describe as mystagogy the teaching that Jesus offered to the crowds, making Jesus a mystagogue and his listeners initiates into the mystery.

---

6. John Chrysostom, *Homily I on the Statues*, 30, *Homilies of St. John Chrysostom*, Nicene and Post-Nicene Fathers, First Series, vol. 9, ed. Philip Schaff, trans. W. R. W. Stephens (Buffalo: Christian Literature Publishing Co., 1889).

7. Gregoriore de Nazianze, *La passion du Christ* 195–96, ed. A. Tuiler, SC 149 (Paris: Cerf, 1969), 145. [My translation from Boselli's Italian.—Trans.]

8. Cyril of Alexandria, *Commentary on the Gospel of Luke*. [My translation from the Italian. Cf. Cyril of Alexandria, *Commentary on the Gospel of Luke*, trans. R. Payne Smith (Oxford, UK: Oxford University Press, 1859), 41, http://www.elpenor.org/cyril-alexandria /luke-commentary.asp?pg=41, accessed January 18, 2014.—Trans.]

When the fathers speak of Jesus as a mystagogue and describe "all that Jesus did and taught from the beginning" (Acts 1:1) as initiation into the mystery of God, they are using extrabiblical categories to describe the extraordinary awareness that John expresses at the conclusion of his gospel: "No one has ever seen God. It is God the only Son, who is close to the Father's heart, who has made him known" (John 1:18). He has "made him known" (*exeghés-ato*): Jesus has offered an exegesis of God. We can therefore describe Jesus, with the Fourth Gospel, as *the exegete of God* and, with the Greek fathers, *the mystagogue of God*, meaning that nothing reveals the mystery of God more than the words and actions of Jesus.

According to the Easter stories of the evangelist Luke, the texts of Scripture are not enough to arouse the disciples' faith in Jesus' resurrection; it is, rather, the Risen One who, manifesting himself to the eleven, "opened their minds to understand the scriptures" (Luke 24:45). The testimony of Easter faith expressed in the gospels tells us that neither the Scriptures nor repetition of the words and gestures of Jesus are sufficient to arouse the church's confession of faith. The risen Christ himself must be the exegete of his mystery hidden in the Scriptures. It is he who opens the minds of the disciples to understand the Scriptures; it is not the Scriptures that open their minds to understand the mystery of Christ. In addition to the testimony of the gospels, and in profound fidelity to them, we have the testimony of the early church, which attests that neither the Scriptures nor the rites, texts, and liturgical gestures are sufficient in themselves to arouse the confession of paschal faith. The Risen One, in the power of the Holy Spirit, is the mystagogue who opens our minds to understand the liturgy. To affirm, in a perspective of faith, that mystagogy is an eminently christological action means therefore to be aware that the intelligence of the believer alone is not enough to understand the mystery hidden in the liturgy. The revelation of the mystery of God is always an act of God, because only the mystery reveals the mystery. Just as every time that the church breaks the bread of the Word it is Christ himself who is the exegete of his mystery contained in the Scriptures, so when the church as mystagogue initiates Christians into the mystery contained in the liturgical action, it is Christ himself who opens their minds to understand the liturgy.

### The Link between the Scriptures and the Liturgy as Matrix of Mystagogy

Having looked at mystagogy as a christological activity, we turn now to consider how the essential link between the Scriptures and the liturgy is the matrix, the womb in which mystagogy has its origins. We considered above the testimony of the Scriptures and the fathers of the church. I would here like to take as a point of departure the witness of the liturgy.

In the most solemn eucharistic celebrations, the Roman Rite calls for the ritual of placing the Book of the Gospels, the Evangelarium, on the altar. It is a gesture of great significance, but one that too often passes nearly unnoticed and is therefore rendered mute and misunderstood. At the beginning of the liturgy, the Evangelarium is carried solemnly, in a grand gesture of being held high before the entire assembly, until reaching the altar, the heart of the assembly. Its enthronement on the altar is truly an epiphany of the mystery, the mystery of the Word of God that, passing through the existence of the people of Israel, finds its realization in the 'avodà, the cultic service offered to God. This cultic service, however, is not the point of arrival of the Word of God but rather the place of the "passage"

of God through the midst of his people; it is intended to permeate the entire existence of the children of Israel, so that their very lives might become the true worship of God.

For us Christians, the same Word that permeated the entire history of Israel, in the fullness of time, "became flesh" (John 1:14) in Jesus Christ. We confess that Jesus is the *'eved Adonaj*, the servant of the Lord who offered his life as a true and total service of God, and for this reason we recognize in him the realization and the fulfillment of the *'avodà*, the true cultic service of God, understood as an offering of oneself, of one's entire life. In Christ, the word of God becomes not just a body but a body offered, a total gift of self. For this reason, the author of the Letter to the Hebrews puts in the mouth of Christ the prophecy of the psalmist:

> Sacrifices and offerings you have not desired,
> but a body you have prepared for me. (Heb 10:5; cf. Ps 40:6)

Behold, then, the epiphany of the mystery in the gesture of placing the Evangelarium upon the altar. The word of God has found its fulfillment in the true worship offered by Christ to God on the cross. It is the gift of self unto death, the body given and the blood poured out, of which the altar is the place of memorial, the place of thanksgiving. Truly profound is the spiritual understanding behind the church's choice to put the enthronement of the Evangelarium on the altar at the very beginning of the eucharistic celebration. It becomes the interpretive key, the hermeneutic of all that is celebrated in the liturgy that has just begun. The gesture is in fact the most eloquent icon with which the liturgy manifests the intrinsic unity that exists between the Scripture and the mystery of the altar, the Eucharist.

The recognition by the fathers of the church of the essential link between the Scriptures and the Eucharist goes as far back as Ignatius of Antioch, who wrote of taking flight "to the gospel as to the flesh of Jesus."[9] For Origen, the words spoken by Christ at the Last Supper over the bread and wine also make reference to the word of Scripture. Origen writes:

> It was not the visible bread that he held in his hands which God the Word called his body, but it was the Word in whose sacrament the bread was to be broken. Nor was it the visible drink that he identified as his blood, but it was the Word in whose sacrament the libation was to be poured out.[10]

Jerome adds:

> [A]s the Lord's flesh is true food and his blood is true drink, on an anagogical level, all the good we have in the present age is to feed on his flesh and drink his blood, not just at the sacrament but also in our reading of the Scriptures.[11]

These few examples are enough to make clear that the fathers of the church recognized a strong relationship between the Scriptures and the Eucharist. It is in this horizon of understanding—the Scriptures and the Eucharist as a single mystery, the sacramental body of Christ—that mystagogy has its origins.

---

9. Ignatius of Antioch, *Letter to the Philadelphians*, 5.1, in Willaim R. Schoedel, *Ignatius of Antioch*, Hermeneia (Philadelphia: Fortress Press, 1985), 200.

10. Origen, *Commentary on Matthew*, in Manlio Simonetti, ed., *Matthew 14–28*, Ancient Christian Commentary on Scripture, NT Ib (Downers Grove, IL: Intervarsity Press, 2002), 248.

11. Jerome, *Commentary on Ecclesiastes*, 3.13, trans. Richard J. Goodrich and David J. D. Miller, Ancient Christian Writers, vol. 66 (New York: Newman Press, 2012), 60.

Until the fourth century, Christians were a persecuted minority, and in these conditions the liturgy was a simple and basic reality. The activity through which the church generated faith was the teaching of the mystery of Christ through commentary on the Scriptures. The spiritual exegesis of the Old and New Testaments was therefore the womb, the matrix in which the church confessed its faith. In the fourth century, the church confronted a new reality, which included the task of leading a great number of catechumens and neophytes to understand the mystery contained in the liturgy. Reading the most ancient mystagogues, it is clear that the fathers intuitively interpreted baptism and Eucharist, and then the liturgy as a whole, in the same way they interpreted the Scriptures, since the Scriptures and the liturgy contain the same mystery: Jesus Christ.

Origen wrote: "The words which have been written are mystical."[12] Elsewhere he said, "[T]he Scriptures were written by the Spirit of God, and have a meaning, not only the meaning that is apparent at first sight, but also another, which escapes the notice of most. For those (words) which are written are the forms of certain mysteries, and the images of divine things."[13] It is clear that the fathers were equally aware that all that the liturgy contains is also mystery and that the liturgical rites too are "the forms of certain mysteries, and the images of divine things." Thus they applied to the liturgy the same exegetical method they used to interpret the Scriptures, the typological method, which they had found used already by the New Testament authors.

12. Origen, *Homilies on Genesis and Exodus*, 10.2, trans. Ronald E. Heine, The Fathers of the Church, vol. 71 (Washington, DC: Catholic University of America Press, 1981), 158.

13. Origen, *De Principiis* 1, ed. Alexander Roberts and James Donaldson, *The Ante-Nicene Fathers*, vol. 4 (New York: Scribners, 1925), 241.

And so Jean Danielou could write, "The application of this [typological] method to Scripture is called spiritual exegesis. When it is applied to the liturgy it is called mystagogy."[14] Typology consisted in understanding the events and people (*týpoi*) of the Old Testament as anticipating and prefiguring the mystery of Christ.

Mystagogy, understood as "typology applied to the liturgy," puts the liturgy in relation to the events of salvation history, as the Old Testament is put in relation to the New. The mystery that the liturgy hides and communicates—the liturgy's "meaning that is not as clear," to paraphrase Origen—is the entire mystery of salvation realized in Christ. However, the typological method applied by the fathers to the liturgy had multiple developments in different ecclesial contexts and schools of exegesis. Over time, mystagogy progressively revealed not only how the liturgy realizes the figures of the Old Testament but also how in every liturgical action there are gestures carried out by Jesus, how it also contains a moral teaching (or an existential value for the life of the believer), and how it prefigures an eschatological reality.

Cyril of Jerusalem, in his mystagogical catechesis on baptism, understands the baptismal anointing as the definitive realization of the anointings narrated in the Old Testament:

> [T]his Chrism is prefigured in the Old Testament. When Moses, conferring on his brother the divine appointment, was ordering him high priest, he anointed him after he had bathed in water, and from that point he was called "Christ" ("anointed"), clearly after the figurative Chrism. . . . But what was done to [him] in figure was done to you, not in figure but in truth, because your salvation

---

14. Jean Danielou, "Le symbolism des rites baptismaux," *Dieu-Vivant* 1 (1945): 17–43 at 17.

began from Him who was anointed by the Holy Spirit in truth.[15]

Through mystagogy the fathers also show that the liturgical action is, in reality, the action of Christ himself and that it is therefore never distinguishable from the action of the Father and the Spirit. Addressing neophytes in baptismal catechesis, John Chrysostom says:

> [I]t is not only the priest who touches the head, but also the right hand of Christ, and this is shown by the very word of the one baptizing. He does not say: "I baptize so-and-so," but: "so-and-so is baptized," showing that he is only the minister of grace and merely offers his hand because he has been ordained to this end by the Spirit. The one fulfilling all things is the Father and the Son and the Holy Spirit, the undivided Trinity.[16]

These extracts of mystagogical texts demonstrate that mystagogy was a true and proper theology of the liturgical mystery, revealing the mystery of Christ and for this reason encompassing a Christian's entire existence. Just as in the Scriptures there is a spiritual meaning hidden within the *graphé*, the human work of writing, so in the liturgy there is a spiritual meaning hidden within the *érgon*, the human action, gesture, or rite. The rite is for the liturgy what letters are for the Scriptures. For this reason, the liturgy, like the Scriptures, calls for a spiritual understanding, a deeper

---

15. Cyril of Jerusalem, *Mystagogical Catecheses* 3, 6, in *The Works of Saint Cyril of Jerusalem*, trans. Leo P. McCauley and Anthony A. Stephenson, *The Fathers of the Church*, vol. 64 (Washington, DC: Catholic University of America Press, 1970), 173.

16. John Chrysostom, *Baptismal Instructions*, 2.26, trans. Paul W. Harkins, Ancient Christian Writers, vol. 31 (Westminster, MD: Newman Press, 1963), 53.

penetration. The more one reads the mystagogical texts, the more it becomes clear that for the fathers, mystagogy was not a simple initiation into the liturgy but rather, starting from the liturgy, an understanding of the single mystery contained in the Scriptures and celebrated in the liturgy: the mystery of Christ. The fathers of the church shared a certainty that *cum Scriptura* and *sub Scriptura* the liturgy had its own way, unique and singular and therefore essential, of communicating the mystery of Christ. The communal prayer of Christians is called *leitourghía*; it is *érgon*, a doing, an acting. The knowledge offered by the liturgy, therefore, is not entirely intellectual and rational. It is an integral knowledge, an experience that invests all of a person's faculties. In the liturgy, one learns by listening, speaking, seeing, smelling, touching. The senses are the pathway to meaning.

## The Relevance of Mystagogy

Mystagogy's relevance to the church today was reiterated forcefully and authoritatively by the Extraordinary Synod of Bishops in 1985, celebrated to mark twenty years since the close of the Second Vatican Council. In its final document, the synod fathers offered several suggestions for the renewal of the liturgy and declared: "Catecheses must once again become paths leading into liturgical life (mystagogical catecheses), as was the case in the Church's beginnings."[17] We should ask ourselves: how far have our churches gone today in the reception and actualization of this invitation? Are we able to say that mystagogical catechesis is penetrating and forming the vital fabric of the Christian community? It is difficult to give a single and

---

17. Final Report of the 1985 Extraordinary Synod, 2.B.b.2, available at http://www.ewtn.com/library/CURIA/SYNFINAL.HTM, accessed January 18, 2014.

definitive response to this question. There are many positive and encouraging signs that give hope, but there are also disheartening and troubling signs, too. We must all, at every level, hold on to the certainty not only of mystagogy's relevance but of its extreme necessity and urgency.

I will limit myself here to recalling two questions found in Scripture. These two questions reveal the permanent relevance of mystagogy, for they demonstrate that it is not an element added on to liturgy but an integral part of the liturgical experience. There is no liturgy without mystagogy. There is no authentic liturgical life without a knowledge of the mystery celebrated in the liturgy.

*"What does this rite of yours mean?"* (Exod 12:26, NABRE)

The Jewish liturgical tradition still lives today and still finds its authenticity confirmed through its obedience to the command found in the book of Exodus:

> Thus, when you have entered the land which the LORD will give you as he promised, you must observe this rite. When your children ask you, "What does this rite of yours mean?" you will reply, "It is the Passover sacrifice for the LORD, who passed over the houses of the Israelites in Egypt; when he struck down the Egyptians, he delivered our houses." (Exod 12:25-27, NABRE)

"What does this rite of yours mean?" is the question addressed at the Jewish Passover by the youngest son to his father who presides. The question is an integral part of the rite itself. Recalling the meaning of the Passover rite, the father's answer protects the rite from the constant risk of standing outside of history. The story he tells prevents the rite from being understood as something magical. Nothing, in fact, is more contrary to the Judeo-Christian faith, a faith in God's actions in history, than the loss of its historicity.[18] And this can happen easily when the liturgical rite is repeated with no knowledge of its meaning.

"What does this rite of yours mean?" is the same question that the ancient church received from its youngest children, the catechumens and neophytes, and the answer is the mystagogical catecheses of the fathers. The fathers demonstrate to Christians that the events of salvation narrated in the Old and New Testaments are present in every liturgical action. Indeed, within the liturgical rite is the most historic thing of all: the entire mystery of the earthly existence of a man, Jesus Christ, his death on the cross and his resurrection, his entire life. If the liturgical rite is not kept constantly united to the historical event from which it was born and of which it is a memorial, it becomes "mute," "inexpressive." It becomes an image that no longer puts us in contact with the living Lord who saved us within history. What is true of the Jewish liturgy is also true of Christian liturgy: when the meaning of the rite is forgotten, contact between the liturgy and salvation history is lost.

The necessity that Christians understand the meaning of their liturgical gestures is affirmed by Origen with a particularly effective image. In his fifth homily on Numbers, Origen explains the spiritual meaning of the Lord's command to Moses and Aaron to ensure that the first group of Levites, the sons of Kohath, are not eliminated (cf. Num 4:18). The specific task of the Kohathites—to whom it was forbidden to enter the Holy of Holies and to see the holy things (that was permitted only to Moses, Aaron, and their sons)—was to carry the ark of the covenant wrapped in leather and with it all the objects of the tent of meeting wrapped in blue cloth. To the Kohathites, then, is given the unique task of carrying on their shoulders the holy things

18. Cf. P. De Benedetti, *La morte de Mosè e altri esempi* (Milan: Bompiani, 1971), 151–54.

wrapped in coverings. Origin sees in the children of Kohath the figure of those Christians who do not know the meaning of the liturgical gestures they perform:

> Who can offer an explanation of the Eucharist, both its overall meaning and the rite that takes place; or of the administration of the baptism: the words, the gestures, the rites, the questions and responses? We bring all these things covered and veiled on our backs, as they were given and entrusted to the high priest and his sons. When we carry out these practices and similar things without knowing the meaning of what we do, we bear a burden on our backs and carry the divine mysteries hidden under cloth.[19]

For Origen, when the meaning of the rites are not known, the mystery remains hidden and becomes a weight that the Christian must bear.

"What does this rite of yours mean?" is the definitive and radical question on the true meaning of the liturgy. Mystagogy is the church's response. It is an essential element of the church's transmission of the true meaning of the liturgy, because it is above all a spiritual understanding of the liturgy that makes transmission of its authentic meaning possible.

*"Do you realize what I have done for you?"* (John 13:12, NABRE)

During the Last Supper, Jesus, in the Fourth Gospel, carries out the gesture of a slave who washes the feet of his master every time the master sits down at table. In the context that John gives it—the Last Supper, which is in the synoptics the place of the Eucharist—and with the sacred gravity with which Jesus performs it, this gesture becomes

---

19. Origin, *Homilies on Numbers* 5.1–4. [My translation from the Italian. –Trans.]

a priestly action that assumes the solemn traits of a liturgical rite. The task of a slave becomes the rite of the Lord. After washing the disciples' feet, Jesus again reclines at table—John tells us—and asks his disciples, "Do you realize what I have done for you?" (John 13:12, NABRE). And then Jesus interprets himself. He becomes the exegete and the mystagogue of his own action: "If I, therefore, the master and teacher, have washed your feet, you ought to wash one another's feet" (John 13:14, NABRE). Just as the entire mystery of Christ, the entire meaning of his existence, is enclosed in the eucharistic gesture of the breaking of the bread and handing over of the cup, so also in the washing of the feet. To understand the meaning of these gestures is to understand Christ.

If, as *Sacrosanctum Concilium* affirms, every liturgical action is an action of Christ,[20] then he still today addresses his question to the church: "Do you realize what I have done for you?" In this question we find the entire relevance of the church's mystagogy for the announcement of the Gospel today. Mystagogy is not one method among other possible methods, not a simple pastoral choice among many; it is the way we know what Christ does today for his church in the liturgy. Just as, for the disciples, understanding the meaning of Jesus washing their feet meant understanding the meaning of his entire life and death, so today, understanding what Christ does in the liturgical action means knowing the mystery of Christ in its entirety. With Christ and the liturgy, there is a circular interpretive movement: knowing Christ through the liturgy because Christ himself is the principle of knowledge and interpretation of the liturgy. Christ is the only and true mystagogue of his mystery. When the church performs mystagogy, it

---

20. Cf. Second Vatican Council, *Sacrosanctum Concilium*, n. 7.

becomes a servant of Christ the mystagogue and makes the Christian an *epóptes*, an eyewitness[21] of the mystery of God. Clement of Alexandria writes:

> For he who is still blind and dumb, not having under-standing, or the undazzled and keen vision of the contem-plative soul, which the Savior confers, like the uninitiated (*amýeteon*) at the mysteries, or the unmusical at dances, not being yet pure and worthy of the pure truth, but still discordant and disordered and material, must stand out-side of the divine choir.[22]

Those who participate in the liturgy without knowing the mystery are like a dancer who dances without knowing the music or the rhythm.

Mystagogy, then, means understanding the mystery nar-rated by the Scriptures and celebrated in the liturgy. Just as the spiritual exegesis of the Scriptures offers under-standing of Christ, so mystagogy, the spiritual exegesis of the liturgy, offers spiritual understanding of Christ. With mystagogy, we can truly apply to the liturgy the well-known principle of Jerome: *Ignoratio Scripturarum, ignoratio Christi est* ("Ignorance of the Scriptures is ignorance of Christ"). In the same way, *Ignoratio liturgiae, ignoratio Christi est* ("Ignorance of the meaning of the liturgy is ignorance of Christ").

---

21. Here we render *epóptes* as eyewitness, as we find it in 2 Peter 1:16. In a more precise sense, the term means "one who sees from above" or "one who contemplates." Of particular interest is how for Plutarch, *epóptes* is one who is initiated into the highest level of the mystery (cf. Plutarch, "Alcibiades" in *The Rise and Fall of Athens: Nine Greek Lives* [New York: Penguin, 1960]).

22. Clement of Alexandria, *The Stromata*, 5.4.

# Chapter Two

# Mystagogy of the Penitential Act

*[O]n the Lord's Day gather to break bread and to give thanks, after having confessed your offenses, so that your sacrifice may be pure.*

—Didache[1]

## "After Having Confessed Your Offenses"

"If we proclaim his death, we proclaim the remission of sins." In this statement, Ambrose summarized a truth that has been confessed by the church's great tradition from the first century up to our own day: the eucharistic celebration is a mystery of forgiveness and reconciliation.[2] Ambrose continues, in his work *On the Sacraments*:

---

1. *Didache* 14.1, in Lawrence J. Johnson, ed., *Worship in the Early Church: An Anthology of Historical Sources*, vol. 1 (Collegeville, MN: Liturgical Press, 2009), 40.

2. This chapter was originally published as "Perdono e reconciliazione nei riti della celebrazione eucaristica: l'atto penitenziale," in *Celebrare la misericordia: "Lasciatevi riconciliare con Dio" (2 Cor 5:20),* ed. Centro di Azione Liturgica (Rome: CLV-Edizione liturgiche, 2010), 121–35.

If we proclaim his death, we proclaim the remission of sins. If whenever his blood is shed, it is shed for the remission of sins, I ought always to receive him so that he may always forgive sins. Since I am always sinning, I always need the medicine.[3]

The entire eucharistic celebration is marked by gestures and words that attest to forgiveness and reconciliation: the penitential act; the *Kyrie*; hearing the word of God proclaimed; the *verba Christi* over the blood that is "poured out for you and for many for the forgiveness of sins";[4] the rite of peace; the Lord's Prayer; the litany of the Lamb of God; the prayers of the priest celebrant; and above all, communion in the holy gifts, the power of which to remit sins is a truth of the tradition attested to by liturgical sources without interruption from the beginning up to the present day. But the most intense and expressive moment in which the individual believer and the assembly together confess their sins and invoke the Lord's mercy is the penitential act, a true and proper liturgy of forgiveness.

The penitential act that opens the eucharistic liturgy is a constitutive and essential moment, and it has had a place there from earliest eucharistic celebrations. It is attested to in the *Didache*, the earliest order of the eucharistic synaxis, bearing witness to the practice of the first generation of Christians in western Syria and Palestine: "[O]n the Lord's Day gather to break bread and to give thanks, after having confessed your offenses, so that your sacrifice may be pure."[5]

---

3. Ambrose of Milan, "Sermons on the Sacraments IV, 28," in Edward Yarnold, *The Awe-Inspiring Rites of Initiation: The Origins of the R.C.I.A.*, 2nd ed. (Collegeville, MN: Liturgical Press, 1994), 139.

4. Eucharistic Prayer I in *The Roman Missal, Third Edition* (Collegeville, MN: Liturgical Press, 2011), 639.

5. *Didache* 14.1, in Johnson, *Worship in the Early Church*, 40.

This suggests that the confession of sins must necessarily precede the breaking of the bread and the offering of thanks. It is the condition by which "your sacrifice may be pure," an allusion to the new covenant sacrifice announced by the prophet Malachi (cf. Mal 1:11).

From this passage of the *Didache* emerge two fundamental elements important to understanding the penitential act as the first liturgical act of the assembly: coming into the Lord's presence and purification from sins. We must note first of all that the meaning of the penitential act is understood fully only in the context of the dynamic of the introductory rites. This dynamic can be expressed in a series of three terms: presence, mercy, glory. From this, we can grasp more deeply the spiritual meaning of the penitential act as a drawing near to the holiness of God and a purification of sins. We recognize more clearly the theological structure of the penitential act and the individual elements that make it up: invitatory, silence, confession of sin, blessing of absolution.

The method of this brief commentary on the penitential act is inspired by the conviction of *Sacrosanctum Concilium* that "it is from the scriptures that . . . [liturgical] actions and signs derive their meaning."[6] In perfect continuity, the *Catechism of the Catholic Church* asserts, in its section on the liturgy, that "[t]he liturgical actions signify what the Word of God expresses."[7] In other words, the meaning of a liturgical action is found in the word of God as it is expressed in Sacred Scripture. If the study of the Bible is, as the council said, "the very soul of sacred theology,"[8] it is also for the same reason the soul of the liturgy. The liturgy is, in fact, the theology of the church.

6. Second Vatican Council, *Sacrosanctum Concilium*, n. 24.

7. *Catechism of the Catholic Church* (Washington, DC: United States Catholic Conference, 1997), n. 1153.

8. Second Vatican Council, *Dei Verbum*, 24.

## The Penitential Act in the Dynamic of the Introductory Rites

The four elements of the eucharistic celebration that make up the introductory rites—the greeting, the penitential act, the doxology, and the collect—cannot be understood in isolation from each other. Rather, they reproduce a precise scriptural dynamic that becomes a liturgical dynamic: presence, mercy, glory. The purpose of the introductory rites is to bring the assembly into the presence of the Lord. Thus, the first authentically liturgical act that the assembly is called to carry out is to approach God's presence.

With the greeting—even the simplest "The Lord be with you"[9]—the celebrant "signifies the presence of the Lord to the assembled community."[10] The liturgy is a mystery of reciprocal presence: the Lord in the midst of his people and the people assembled before the Lord. *"Nos dignos habuisti astare coram te et tibi ministrare,"*[11] the second eucharistic prayer proclaims: "you have held us worthy to be in your presence and minister to you,"[12] and the one who presides says it in the name of the entire priestly assembly.

In the vision of both the Scriptures and the liturgy, coming into the presence of the Lord means first of all considering one's own worthiness. The author of Psalm 24 asks, in a hymn composed for the liturgical entry into the temple of Jerusalem:

9. *The Roman Missal*, 514.

10. *General Instruction of the Roman Missal*, n. 50, in *The Roman Missal*, 30.

11. *Missale Romanum*, Editio typical tertia (Vatican City: Libreria Editrice Vaticana, 2002, emendata 2008), 582.

12. Eucharistic Prayer II, in *The Roman Missal*, 648.

> Who shall ascend the hill of the LORD?
> And who shall stand in his holy place? (Ps 24:3)

The response comes: "Those who have clean hands and pure hearts" (Ps 24:4). Only those whose hands and hearts—that is, whose actions and interiority—are pure can stand in the presence of the Holy One. By evoking the purification of hands and heart, we are immediately reminded of the words of the *Confiteor*: "I have greatly sinned, in my thoughts and in my words, in what I have done and in what I have failed to do."[13] In these words, one finds an authentic liturgical anthropology. All of the faculties of one's freedom, intelligence, and action are brought together in the confession of sin, so that we say, paraphrasing Psalm 24, "I have sinned in my heart (thought), with my mouth (words), and with my hands (works and omissions)."

In the Scriptures, the pure and just one is not the one who is without sin but the one who recognizes his sin. This helps us understand the meaning of the invitation that the celebrant offers to the assembly: "Brothers and sisters, let us acknowledge our sins, and so prepare ourselves to celebrate the sacred mysteries."[14] "*Fratres, agnoscamus peccata nostra,*"[15] the Latin text reads, indicating that the first act to which the assembly is called, once it has gathered in the presence of God, is to acknowledge its own condition of sinfulness, making its own the experience of the *Miserere* psalm: "*Iniquitatem meam ego cognosco,*" "I know my transgressions" (Ps 51:5 NABRE). The just one, then, is the sinner who knows her own sinfulness.

13. *The Roman Missal*, 515.
14. Ibid.
15. *Missale Romanum*, 505.

Having been forgiven of its sins, the assembly is then worthy to offer its praise to God by singing the Gloria. This sequence—invocation of God's mercy and proclamation of God's glory—expresses a fundamental biblical truth regarding the relationship between the mercy and the glory of God. According to the rabbinical tradition, the *Shekinah*, the sacramental presence of God in the midst of his people, is manifested above all in the mercy God offers in response to the infidelities of the Israelites.

Through the sin of idolatry committed by the adoration of the golden calf, Israel broke its covenant with the Lord. In Exodus 33 and 34, the celebration of the renewal of this covenant between God and Israel includes the manifestation of the glory of God as mercy. On Mount Sinai, Moses asks the Lord, "Show me your glory" (Exod 33:18), that is, show your *kavod*, your power in history, your identity.

> The Lord descended in the cloud and stood with him there, and proclaimed the name, "The Lord." The Lord passed before him and proclaimed,
> "The Lord, the Lord,
> a God merciful and gracious,
> slow to anger,
> and abounding in steadfast love and faithfulness,
> keeping steadfast love for the thousandth generation,
> forgiving iniquity and transgression and sin."
>     (Exod 34:5-7a)

To Moses who asked, "Show me your glory," the Lord proclaims his name, that is, his identity that determines his action in history. He is the "merciful and gracious" God who "forgiv[es] iniquity and transgression and sin."

Made pure by the mercy of God, the liturgical assembly is worthy to worship, and by singing the Gloria it expresses its intention to carry out the act of worship in its totality, evoking the five fundamental cultic verbs of the Bible:

> We praise you,
> we bless you,
> we adore you,
> we glorify you,
> we give you thanks for your great glory.[16]

The fullness of worship is always in itself the fullness of faith, represented here in the doxological confession of the Tri-unity of God in whose presence the assembly gathers:

> For you alone the Holy One,
> you alone are the Lord,
> you alone are the Most High,
> Jesus Christ,
> with the Holy Spirit
> in the glory of God the Father.[17]

And so the triple confession is complete: *confessio presentiae, confessio peccatorum, confessio gloriae.* The collect, finally, is a prayerful synthesis of all this: the assembly turns to the Lord and calls on him.

The church has always understood this meaning of the introductory rites, even in the era of *devotio moderna*, which was marked by a great distance between spirituality and liturgy. Francis de Sales, in his *Introduction to the Devout Life*, recommends, "From the beginning until the priest goes up to the altar, make your preparation with him. This consists in placing yourself in the presence of God, recognizing your unworthiness, and asking pardon

16. *The Roman Missal*, 522.
17. Ibid.

for your sins."[18] Having considered the meaning of the introductory rites, we now turn to considering the spiritual meaning of the penitential act: drawing near to the holiness of God and the purification of sin.

## *The Spiritual Meaning*

The apostle Paul describes Christians as "called [by God] to be holy" (Rom 1:7, NABRE). The liturgical assembly is also called to be holy, through God's call and in no other way. It is not the location of the assembly that determines its holiness. It can gather anywhere, in a cathedral or a piazza, in a sanctuary or a stadium. The assembly is holy because the risen Lord is in its midst, according to his promise, "[W]here two or three are gathered in my name, I am there among them" (Matt 18:20). For this reason, the church, whose most fundamental epiphany is the liturgical assembly, understands itself, in coming into the Lord's presence, to be, as *Lumen Gentium* affirms, "*sancta simul et semper purificanda*,"[19] both holy and always in need of purification. Every Christian shares the experience of being both holy by the call of God and sinful by condition.

Every time we draw near to the Lord in the liturgy, then, it is as though in the penitential act we respond symbolically to God's command to Moses from the burning bush: "Come no closer! Remove the sandals from your feet, for the place on which you are standing is holy ground" (Exod 3:5). The vocabulary of the entire episode of the burning bush is full of cultic resonance. The place where the bush

18. Francis de Sales, *Introduction to the Devout Life*, trans. John K. Ryan (New York: Image, 1972, 1989), 104.

19. Second Vatican Council, *Lumen Gentium* n. 8, in *Enchiridion vaticanum I*, 483.

burns is described as *admat qodesh*, literally a "land of holiness," in the sense of being a place set apart, in the same way the temple area was "holy space." The Targum comments, "[Before the burning bush] Moses hid his face because he was afraid to look on *the Glory of the Shekinah of the Lord*."[20]

God's insistence that Moses come no closer makes him aware of being in a place made holy by God's presence, and for this reason he must remove his sandals. Augustine asked, "What are the sandals?" and answered:

> What are shoes? Well, what *are* the shoes we wear? Leather from dead animals. The hides of dead animals are what we protect our feet with. So what are we being ordered to do? To give up dead works. This is symbolically what he instructs Moses to do in his honor, where the Lord says to him, *Take off your shoes. For the place you are standing in is holy ground* (Exod 3:5). There's no holier ground than the Church of God, is there? So as we stand in her let us take off our shoes, let us give up dead works.[21]

The act of removing sandals imposed on Moses is therefore a symbol of the interior dispositions that are required of all who wish to, in their worship, approach the presence of God and adore. "To renounce the works of death," Augustine says; drawing near to the holiness of God requires breaking our attachments to all that is of the world, so that we will not bring the filth of sin and idolatry into the holy place.

20. Targum on Exodus 3:6, in *Targum Neofiti 1: Exodus*, *The Aramaic Bible*, vol. 2, trans. Martin McNamara (Collegeville, MN: Liturgical Press, 1994), 18.

21. Augustine of Hippo, Sermon 100.7, in *Sermons*, part 3, vol. 4, trans. Edmund Hill (Brooklyn: New City Press, 1992), 68.

When God calls those who believe in him into his presence, he calls them above all to leave behind what is of the world and to approach his holiness. The penitential act responds precisely to this call. The apostle Paul teaches that Christians have "died with Christ to the elemental powers of the world" (Col 2:20, NABRE), and for this reason are no longer "enslaved to the elemental powers of the world" (Gal 4:3, NABRE). If Christ has said to his disciples, "[Y]ou do not belong to the world, but I have chosen you out of the world" (John 15:19; cf. 17:11-16), Christians must be aware that this is never more true than in the liturgy. The liturgical action makes us, sacramentally, in the world but not of the world.

But the decisive passing from worldliness to holiness comes through purification from sin, the work of God's mercy. The penitential act at the beginning of the eucharistic celebration attests that every time the believer stands, in the liturgy, in God's holy presence, he is called to relive spiritually the experience of the prophet Isaiah in the temple of Jerusalem (see Isa 6:1-8). During the evening incense offering, the prophet receives the vision of the solemn heavenly liturgy. He sees the Lord attended by seraphim who proclaim to one another:

> Holy, holy, holy is the Lord of hosts;
> The whole earth is full of his glory. (Isa 6:3)

In the liturgical hymn known as the *Trisagion*, the words *holiness* and *glory* resonate insistently, and Isaiah avers that he is a sinner, that in him there is neither glory nor holiness but only impurity that renders him both radically other than God and intimately one with the sin of his people. He is not the only just one in Israel; he is a sinner like all people, and for this he exclaims: "Woe is me! I am lost, for I am a man of unclean lips, and I live among a people of unclean lips" (Isa 6:5).

While his words are correctly translated as "I am lost," it is helpful to note that the verb form *nidmeti* (perfect *nif'al* of the verb *damah*) can also mean "I am reduced to silence" (from the root *d m h*), "I am struck speechless." The prophet is struck speechless before the vision of the Lord. It reduces him to silence. Before the epiphany of God, he must fall silent. This is the necessary condition for disposing oneself to hear God's word. But in exclaiming "I am reduced to silence," it is as though the prophet Isaiah also recognizes the impossibility of joining in the singing of the seraphim as they confess God's holiness. Isaiah must acknowledge being unable to confess in truth the glory of God and so add his voice to those of the seraphim because he is "a man of unclean lips."

Isaiah continues his account of the vision: "Then one of the seraphs flew to me, holding a live coal that had been taken from the altar with a pair of tongs. The seraph touched my mouth with it and said, 'Now that this has touched your lips, your guilt has departed and your sin is blotted out'" (Isa 6:6-7). The fire from the altar purifies the prophet's lips; the burning coal has the effect of a sacrificial offering, which is always expiation of sins, forgiveness, purification, and reconciliation. The prophet is left purified by the fire, his sins consumed, and now he is worthy to actively participate in that liturgy of which he was until that moment only a spectator. "Here I am; send me!" Isaiah cries out (Isa 6:8), responding to the call of the Lord.

Like Isaiah, believers who approach God's presence in the liturgy become aware of being reduced to silence, struck speechless, doomed, annihilated, because they are people "of unclean lips, [who] live among a people of unclean lips." The penitential act at the beginning of the liturgy insists on an initial purification as the condition of being in the presence of God, that one may "celebrate [worthily] the sacred mysteries"[22] and unite one's own voice to that of the liturgy of heaven. God's forgiveness consumes every sin. It reaches out and touches every believer as the angel touched the prophet's mouth with the burning coal, to purify her and conform her to the holiness of God. Turning away from one's sins, one hears and responds again to the call to be holy.

Of great interest here is the liturgical exegesis of Isaiah's vision offered by the East Syrian liturgy, in the anaphora of Theodore of Mopsuestia, one of the church's oldest eucharistic prayers. Throughout the singing of the *Trisagion* hymn by the assembly, with each cry of "Holy," the celebrant makes a metania and a genuflection, reciting a *Kusapa*, which puts on his lips a composition that weaves together the words spoken by the prophet before the vision of God's glory in Isaiah 6 with those pronounced by Jacob in Genesis 28 after awaking from his dream of the stairway between heaven and earth, on which he sees angels ascending and descending:

> Woe to me, woe to me, I am wretched, because I am a man of unclean lips and live in the midst of a people of impure lips, and my eyes have seen the king, the Lord almighty. How terrible is this place, since today, I have seen the Lord. And here there is no one at the entrance of the house of God or at the door of heaven.[23]

This Syrian anaphora connects the liturgical action of the celebrant with the spiritual experience of the encounter with God experienced by Isaiah in his temple vision and

22. *The Roman Missal*, 515.

23. Anaphora of Theodore of Mopsuestia, in *Segno di unità. Le più antiche eucaristie delle chiese*, ed. E. Mazza and the Monastics of Bose (Bose: Qiqajon, 1996), 310. [My translation from the Italian.—Trans.]

by Jacob in his dream of the stairway. Superimposed, the biblical episodes and the liturgical actions are identified with one another and interpret one another. The result is that in the eucharistic celebration, which is the memorial of the sacrifice of Christ, the epiphanies of God narrated in the Law and the Prophets are realized again today.

This eucharistic interpretation of Isaiah 6 does not belong uniquely to the Eastern liturgical sources. It is also found in the West, in the old Mozarabic liturgy. In the *illatio* (equivalent of the Roman *praefatio*) of the *Missa sanctorum Fausti, Ianuarii et Martialis*, the link between the burning coals in the vision of Isaiah and the Eucharist is articulated in an especially original way. One reads in the central part of the *illatio*:

> Offering a sacrifice of praise worthy of your majesty in honor of these martyrs, we ask that the holocaust placed on this altar be sanctified by the sign of your Son, by the descent of the Holy Spirit, by the presence of the angel who is your messenger. May it be accepted by you, may it be welcomed by you, may it be for you holy, venerable, glorious, abundant, and living, vital and aflame. May each one of us who eat of it become that burning ember which the prophet Isaiah saw taken from the altar with a tong. Purify our unclean lips, sanctify our hearts soiled by sins. May it be life for the believer, pardon for those who confess [their sins], joy for the afflicted, health for the sick, ointment of refreshment for the tired. May it be life for those afraid of death, a right path for those returning from error, and may you, Lord, who have strengthened the weakness of our spirit and the infirmity of our flesh, be our holy and everlasting medicine.[24]

---

24. *Le "Liber mozarabicus sacramentorum" et les manuscrits mozarabes*, ed. M. Ferotin (Rome: CLV- Edizioni liturgiche, 1995), 402. [My translation from the Italian.—Trans.]

The first thing to notice, with respect to the Eastern tradition, is how in this text of the *vetus hispanica* the burning embers are not simply a eucharistic image. Rather, those who are nourished by the Eucharist become themselves "that burning ember which the prophet Isaiah saw taken from the altar with a tong," and so are purified of sins.

"[G]ive thanks, after having confessed your offenses, so that your sacrifice may be pure,"[25] says the *Didache*, recalling the new covenant sacrifice foretold by Malachi (cf. Mal 1:11). In the old sacrificial economy, the purity of the animal victim was the *conditio sine qua non* that one's sacrificial offering might be accepted by God; in Christianity, what the believer offers in sacrifice is his or her own life which, in communion with Christ the "lamb without defect or blemish" (1 Pet 1:19), must also be a *"hostiam puram, hostiam sanctam, hostiam immaculatam,"*[26] according to the formula of the Roman Canon. This explains the admonishment with which the *Didache* concludes its action of thanksgiving:

> If anyone is holy, let him come;
> If anyone is not, let him do penance.
> Maranatha.[27]

The liturgy of the penitential act is for believers a decisive moment in which the spiritual experience of reconciliation with God and of approaching his presence is brought into our own lives, realizing in the present the purpose of the work accomplished by God in Christ: "[God] has now reconciled in his fleshly body through death, so as to present you holy and blameless and irreproachable before him" (Col 1:22).

---

25. *Didache* 14.1, in Johnson, *Worship in the Early Church*, 40.
26. *Missale Romanum*, 576–77.
27. *Didache* 5.6, in Johnson, *Worship in the Early Church*, 38.

## The Theological Structure

The structure of the penitential act at the opening of the eucharistic celebration reproduces exactly the structure of the principle penitential liturgies of the Israelite community narrated by the Bible, each of which are composed of four elements: invitatory, silence, confession, blessing.[28]

These penitential liturgies are presided over by the head of the community of Israel, who calls the people together to do penance. The prophetic call to conversion found in the prophet Joel is inspired by the literary genre of invitation to penitential liturgy:[29]

> [R]eturn to me with all your heart,
> with fasting, with weeping, and with mourning;
> rend your hearts and not your clothing.
> Return to the LORD, your God,
> for he is gracious and merciful,
> slow to anger, and abounding in steadfast love,
> and relents from punishing. (Joel 2:12-13)

In the same way, the penitential act opens with a formula that invites the assembly to repentance: "Brothers and sisters, let us acknowledge our sins, and so prepare ourselves to celebrate the sacred mysteries."[30]

The Italian edition of the Missal offers some optional introductory formulas that are rich in liturgical and spiritual insight and that are examples of successful liturgical exegesis. Each of these invitatory formulas places the assembly, spiritually, within the setting of a gospel passage.

---

28. Cf. Exod 9:3–10:1; Neh 9:1-37; Bar 1–2. On this assertion, see E. Lipinski, *La liturgie pénitentielle dans la Bible* (Paris: Cerf, 1969).

29. Ibid., 25.

30. *The Roman Missal*, 515.

One places the assembly into Luke's story of the tax collector in the temple (see Luke 18:9-14), making the tax collector's humility and penance the model for approaching God:

> Humble and repentant, like the tax collector in the temple,
> we draw near to God who is just and holy,
> because he forgives our sins.

Another formula places the assembly in the context of the Johannine story of the woman caught in adultery (see John 8:1-11). Calling those assembled to acknowledge their sin and inviting them to forgive one another, it exhorts them to assume the attitude opposite of those who condemned the adulteress in the gospel episode:

> The Lord said: Let the one among you who is without sin
> be the first to throw a stone.
> We recognize ourselves as sinners and we forgive one another
> from the depths of our hearts.

This scriptural episode recounts the spiritual experience of being alone with one's sins before the Lord, living the same condition that the adulteress lived: "Jesus was left alone with the woman standing before him" (John 8:9). Augustine comments: *"Relicti sunt duo, misera et misericordia"* ("The two were left alone, the wretched woman and Mercy").[31] These two realities—humanity's misery and God's mercy—stand face-to-face in the penitential act. Even when the presider introduces the penitential rite more spontaneously, his words must evoke a scriptural

---

31. St. Augustine, Tractate 33.5, in *Homilies on the Gospel of John*, ed. Philip Schaff, Nicene and Post-Nicene Fathers, vol. 7 (Grand Rapids, MI: Eerdmans, 1991), 198.

scene or passage that invites the assembly to share such a spiritual attitude.

The second element of the penitential act, equally essential, is silence. In the penitential rites narrated in the Bible, ritual silence represents the recognition of a sad and deplorable situation. The prophet Zechariah calls the children of Israel to penance with an invitation to silence: "Be silent, all people, before the Lord" (Zech 2:13). The silence of the penitential act is intense, austere, severe. In the liturgy, in fact, silence assumes different functions and meanings according to the context in which it is placed, and for good reason John Chrysostom said, "In the Grecian mysteries there are dancings, but in ours, silence and decency, modesty, and bashfulness."[32]

After silence comes the communal confession of sins. Though there is much to consider on this topic in the Bible, it is enough to recall here the formula that Jeremiah repeats several times: "we have sinned against the Lord our God, we and our ancestors" (Jer 3:25; cf. 14:19-22). Though the Missal presents three possible formulas of confession of sin, I will consider here only the *Confiteor*, which is certainly the one most typical of the Roman rite, if not the one most used. It is enough to recall here the decisive role that this pearl of the *lex orandi* played in supporting the legitimacy of the church's *mea culpa* expressed by Pope John Paul II during the Great Jubilee of the year 2000. The *Confiteor* was one of the major liturgical arguments offered by then-Cardinal Ratzinger to demonstrate the consistency of the pope's act with the church's *regula fidei*. In

---

32. St. John Chrysostom, "Homily 12 on Colossians," in *Homilies on Galatians, Ephesians, Philippians, Colossians, Thessalonians, Timothy, Titus, and Philemon*, ed. Philip Schaff, Nicene and Post-Nicene Fathers, vol. 13 (Grand Rapids, MI: Eerdmans, 1994), 318.

addressing the issue, the cardinal offered a true theological commentary on the *Confiteor*:

> The newspapers speak rightly of the pope's *mea culpa* in the name of the church, and here one can cite a liturgical prayer, the *Confiteor*, which is part of the liturgy each day. The priest, the pope, the laity together, in their "I"—every individual and the entire church—acknowledge before God and in the presence of their brothers and sisters having sinned, of bearing guilt, even great guilt. Two aspects of this beginning of the sacred liturgy seem to me to be important here. On one hand, one speaks of the "I." "I" have sinned, and I do not confess the sins of others. I don't confess the anonymous sins of the collective. I confess with my "I." But at the same time, it is all of the members who with their "I" say "I have sinned." The entire living church in all its living members says "I have sinned" . . . The subject of this confession is "I." I don't confess the sins of others, but my own sins. But on the second point, the "I" confesses, but does so in communion with others. Aware of this communion, one confesses before God but asks the prayers of one's brothers and sisters—that is, seeks in this common confession before God a common reconciliation.[33]

The penitential act concludes with a fixed formula called "absolution":[34]

---

33. Joseph Ratzinger, "La colpa della chiesa. Presentazione del document 'Memoria e riconciliazione' della Commissione teologica internazionale," in idem, *Vi ho chiamato amici. La compagnia nel cammino della fide* (Cinisello Balsamo: San Paolo, 2006), 86–87.

34. *General Instruction of the Roman Missal* 51, in *The Roman Missal*, 30; The *Catechism of the Catholic Church* clarifies the teaching of the GIRM on this point: "The Eucharist is not ordered to the forgiveness of mortal sins—that is proper to the sacrament of Reconciliation" (*Catechism of the Catholic Church*, n. 1395).

May almighty God have mercy on us,
forgive us our sins,
and bring us to everlasting life.[35]

Biblically, this formula is a blessing in which the forgiveness of sins is given. It corresponds exactly to the priestly blessing that concludes the penitential liturgies of the Bible. In this blessing, the name of the Lord is pronounced over the assembly. In this name, the forgiveness of sins is given. It is therefore a true and proper absolution. Similarly, at the end of the liturgy of *Yom Kippur*, the high priest gave the people the blessing in which was pronounced the holy name of the Lord with the formula of Exodus 34:6, which we have already cited:

The LORD, the LORD,
a God merciful and gracious,
slow to anger,
and abounding in steadfast love and faithfulness.

Our penitential act, too, concludes with a blessing in which the forgiveness of sins is given by pronouncing over the assembly the holy name of God and invoking God's attributes: mercy, compassion, omnipotence, holiness.

## Sacramental Efficacy

Although called "absolution," the blessing that concludes the penitential act—the GIRM explains—"lacks the efficacy of the Sacrament of Penance."[36] The meaning of this clarification is understood fully if it is interpreted in the light of

---

35. *The Roman Missal*, 515.
36. *General Instruction of the Roman Missal*, n. 51, in *The Roman Missal*, 30.

the apostle Paul's exhortation to the Christians of Corinth on the necessity to receive the body of Christ worthily:

> Whoever, therefore, eats the bread or drinks the cup of the Lord in an unworthy manner [*anaxios*] will be answerable for the body and blood of the Lord. Examine yourselves, and only then eat of the bread and drink of the cup. For all who eat and drink without discerning the body, eat and drink judgment against themselves. (1 Cor 11:27-29)

For Paul, communion in the bread and the chalice of the Lord requires a prior discernment of the quality of one's relationship with God and with one's brothers and sisters, that is, of whether the act of sacramental communion is contradicted by a grave situation of existential noncommunion with God and with the church. What meaning would there be for someone who is, in daily living, separated from God and from his brothers and sisters in faith (thus demonstrating a failure to discern the body of the Lord) to nourish himself on that bread that "makes the church"? This is the reason for the severe apostolic admonishment, which has become for the church the criterion for participation at the eucharistic table.

Origen sees such criterion expressed already in some way in Jesus' act of healing the sick before the multiplication of the loaves of bread. He finds in this episode the reason for the necessity of the purification from sin as condition for receiving the Eucharist:

> [F]irst observe that when he was about to give to the disciples the loaves of blessing, that they might set them before the multitudes, [Jesus] healed the sick, in order that, having been restored to health, they might participate in the loaves of blessing; for while they are yet sickly, they are not able to receive the loaves of the blessing of Jesus. But if any one, when he ought to listen to the pre-

cept, "But let each prove himself, and so let him eat of the bread," etc., does not obey these words, but in haphazard fashion participates in the bread of the Lord and His cup, he becomes weak or sickly, or even— if I may use the expression— on account of being stupefied by the power of the bread, asleep.[37]

Theodore of Mopsuestia, in attesting to the purifying power of the Eucharist, indicates with still greater precision the criteria with which to discern the gravity of sins:

Sins of human weakness should not restrain us from partaking in the holy mystery. . . . We should therefore neither stay away completely nor carelessly approach the mysteries, but we must strive with all our power to lead a good life. So doing, may we hasten to Communion, knowing that if our lives are careless, if we sin without fear, if we do whatever we please, then it is unto condemnation that we eat and drink this ineffable food and drink. But if we show concern for how we live our lives and strive to do what is good, if we always reflect upon this in our hearts, then our involuntary sins, those resulting from human weakness, will not harm us. On the other hand, we will profit greatly from receiving the mysteries. The Body and Blood of our Lord and the grace of the Holy Spirit given by the sacrament will strengthen us in doing good and fortify our dispositions, repelling all evil thoughts and removing sins—presuming that these have been committed involuntarily or out of human weakness. . . . If we sin through carelessness, it will go hard for us should we approach the holy mysteries. But if we zealously do good, avoid evil, and sincerely repent of our sins, then the holy mysteries will be the gift of the forgiveness of sins. . . . If we are guilty of a great sin against

37. Origen, "Commentary on the Gospel of Matthew 10:25," in *The Ante-Nicene Fathers*, vol. 9 (New York: Scribner's, 1925), 431.

the Law—the type of sin being unimportant—we must refrain from Communion and yet not stay away indefinitely. What good does it do to continue on in the same sins? We must make every effort to move our conscience so that we are eager to do penance for sins. The priests and experts who treat and care for sinners are to follow the Church's discipline and wisdom in healing penitents, this being regulated according to the seriousness of a person's sins.[38]

There are then sins that are the fruit of "human weakness" that do not impede our access to the holy mysteries, which give the strength to combat and to overcome every weakness. Other sins, which Theodore speaks of as "great sin[s]," are an obstacle to eucharistic communion and require a journey of penitence and of pastoral care by a spiritual guide who "follow[s] the Church's discipline and wisdom."

Summing up, it is completely incorrect to deny all sacramental value to the prayer of absolution recited at the end of the penitential act, since every formula and gesture of the liturgy possesses a sacramental quality. Indeed, to suggest that the words of forgiveness spoken by the priest do not effect what they signify, being merely a simple greeting or formality, would gravely contradict the meaning of the liturgy and the value of the words spoken within it. By specifying instead that the absolution "lacks the efficacy of the Sacrament of Penance,"[39] the GIRM demonstrates both liturgical insight and pastoral wisdom while remaining in continuity with the great tradition of the church to

38. Theodore of Mopsuestia, *Homily* 16: 33, 34, 39, in Johnson, *Worship in the Early Church*, vol. 3, 273–75.

39. *General Instruction of the Roman Missal*, n. 51, in *The Roman Missal*, 30.

which the patristic texts cited above attest. The GIRM does not affirm that the absolution of the penitential act lacks sacramental efficacy but that it "lacks the efficacy of the Sacrament of Penance" (*"quae tamen effacacia sacramenti paenitentiae caret"*). The absolution enjoys a different level of efficacy, certainly inferior to the sacrament of penance.

Recognizing the place of the sacrament of penance for forgiving the sins that shatter one's communion with God and with the church does not dismiss, much less negate, the effective and real forgiveness of God given in the penitential act. Rather, it is for the believer a moment of standing before God and assessing our own actions, recognizing even our "great sins," to use the expression of Theodore of Mopsuestia. The efficacy of any sacrament, whichever one it may be, can never be reduced to a simple formula that is recited. Indeed, the efficacy of a sacrament, like that of the Word of God, is more intense to the extent that the one receiving it is aware of her own spiritual condition and generously disposed to receive and respond to the gift of grace. To acknowledge that forgiveness of a "great sin" requires the sacrament of penance means to affirm the necessity of a period of conversion and penance in which the believer is helped by a spiritual guide to become aware of his existential situation. This journey is the sacrament of penance, above all when it is understood and celebrated in its full expression. This is where the proper and exclusive efficacy of the sacrament of penance is to be found.

Therefore, the church's understanding of the meaning and the value of the absolution that concludes the penitential act both guards the true meaning of discernment of communion in the body and the blood of Christ and attests to a wise pastoral and spiritual pedagogy toward the believer who is in sin. Faithful to the great tradition of the church, this understanding in no way denies that the forgiveness of God proclaimed and conferred at the conclusion of the penitential act is sacramental; with real efficacy, this act achieves what it proclaims and signifies.

Thanks to the Missal of Paul VI, the penitential act is an action of the entire assembly. Here we see one of the fundamental successes of the great postconciliar liturgical reform. It comes as the result of that drinking from the genuine sources of Christianity, the Bible and the fathers of the church, which was the great work of the council and also of the liturgical reform that followed it.

A fine synthesis of the mystagogical journey we have traveled here is the formula of the Syriac liturgy, with which the celebrant dismisses the assembly:

> Go in peace, beloved brothers; we entrust you to the grace and the mercy of the holy Trinity, and to the viaticum that you have taken from the purifying altar of the Lord, all of you, near and far, living and dead, saved by the glorious cross of the Lord and signed by the sign of holy baptism. May the holy Trinity forgive your errors, remit your sins, and give you the repose of your soul at your deaths. Have pity on me, a weak and sinful servant, with the help of your prayers. Go in peace, content and joyful, and pray for me.[40]

40. *Messale della Divina Liturgia della chiesa siro-ortodossa de Antiochia* (Milan, 1999), 74. [My translation from the Italian.—Trans.]

# Chapter Three

# Mystagogy of the Liturgy of the Word

> *Blessed is that congregation of which Scripture testifies that "the eyes of all were fixed on him"!*
>
> —Origen[1]

## *Jesus, the Word Who Reads the Scriptures*

Jesus reads the Scriptures only one time in the gospels, and he does it in the context of a liturgy.[2] In the synagogue of Nazareth, in the midst of the assembly gathered in prayer for the Sabbath, Jesus reads the prophecy of Isaiah and comments on it (cf. Luke 4:16-21). According to the gospel texts, those who gathered in that synagogue are the only people ever to have seen and heard Jesus read the Scriptures aloud in a liturgical assembly. How blessed these

1. Origen, Homily 32.6, in *Homilies on Luke*, trans. Joseph T. Lienhard (Washington, DC: Catholic University of America Press, 1996), 133.

2. This chapter was originally published as *Leggere le Scritture nella liturgia*, Sentieri di senso 4 (Bose: Qiqajon, 2010).

people to have heard with their own ears *the Word reading Scripture!*

In the Gospel of Luke, Jesus begins his preaching ministry with that reading, and so his first ministerial act is an act of worship. His first public gesture is a liturgical gesture. He marks the beginning of his ministry not in the temple offering sacrifice but in a synagogue reading the Scriptures. He opens his mission by opening the scroll of the prophet and reading: "The Spirit of the Lord GOD is upon me" (Isa 61:1). The Spirit who descended upon Jesus at his baptism in the Jordan (cf. Luke 3:22) not only guided Jesus into the desert (cf. Luke 4:1) but also then guided him to read from the scroll of the prophet, demonstrating that the epiclesis of the Spirit always accompanies the reading of the Scriptures and inspires their interpretation.

The opening of this reading from the prophet becomes the beginning of Jesus' presentation of himself to his followers as a prophet, leaving them surprised and incredulous at his words. By reading this liturgical pericope, he manifests himself as the Messiah. And so what happens in the synagogue of Nazareth is at the same time liturgy, epiphany, and theophany, because in that insignificant hamlet on the outskirts of Israel, the Nazarene brings to fulfillment that which, according to the Letter to the Hebrews, the Christ confesses as he enters the world: "in the scroll of the book it is written of me" (Heb 10:7; cf. Ps 40:7). "*In capite libri scriptum est de me*," is the way Jerome translates the Greek text of the psalm (*en kephalídi biblíou*). Christ is the *caput libri*, the text, the beginning of the book in which the will of the Father is written. For this reason, as a medieval author once wrote, the incarnate Son is the *liber maximus*, the pages of which are his flesh: "He [Christ] is the book whose parchment is flesh and whose writing is the Father's Word. . . . The greatest book is the incarnate Son."[3] Similarly, an unedited Stutt-gardian manuscript calls him "a book of intense colors":

> The Son of God is a book of intense colors. This precious book is never closed, its pages never yellow with age. It is just as legible at night as it is during the day. It is a book of immense value, a book of great purity; a book for all times, to read and entrust to one's heart.[4]

What happens in the Nazareth synagogue liturgy is the institution of the Liturgy of the Word, its *týpos*, in the very same way that the institution of the Christian eucharistic celebration happened in the upper room in Jerusalem, at the Last Supper. And so the Christian reading of Scripture and the Eucharist were instituted by him in the same way. That is, by taking in his hands the scroll of Isaiah, Jesus initiated the *novum testamentum*, just as by taking in his hands the cup at the supper he gave the *calix novi testament* (see Luke 22:20). In Nazareth, the Word read the Scripture, and from that day, from that "today" (Luke 4:21), the reading offered by Jesus became the way Christians read the Scriptures.[5] Just as Christ read the Isaiah passage and interpreted it by identifying what in it "is written of me" (Ps 40:7), Christians have read and understood the Scriptures of Israel in their liturgical assemblies,

3. R. Bornert, *Les commentaires byzantins de la Divine liturgie du VII^e au XV^e siècle* (Paris: Institut français d'etudes byzantines, 1966), 29.

4. Cited in Jean Leclerq, "Lectio Divina: Jésus Livre et Jésus Lecteur," in *Collectanea cisterciensia* 47 (1986): 210–11.

5. Charles Perrot sees in the account of Luke 4:16-21 a reflection of the first Christian communities' practice of proclaiming the Scriptures: "The hellenist-Christian church of Luke already practiced a directly christological kind of communal reading" ("Jésus, le lecteur des Écritures," *Théophilyon* 1 [2001], 84).

always finding "in the law of Moses, the prophets, and the psalms" (Luke 24:44) "what referred to him" (Luke 24:27, NABRE). The Christian reading of Scripture was accomplished first by Christ, and so he is the *caput libri* of the New Testament. Looking closer, the admonition "I have set you an example, that you also should do as I have done to you" (John 13:15) applies not only to Jesus washing the feet of the twelve but also to the reading and interpretation of the Scriptures that the risen Jesus accomplished for the disciples when "beginning with Moses and all the prophets, he interpreted to them what referred to him in all the scriptures" (Luke 24:27, NABRE).

It is only by following this example of Christ that the church can confess—as it did at the Second Vatican Council—that "it is he himself [Christ] who speaks when the holy scriptures are read in church,"[6] and "in the liturgy God speaks to his people, and Christ is still proclaiming his gospel."[7] These passages, among the most important and authoritative of the conciliar magisterium on the word of God in the life of the church, express the authentic meaning of the church's faith in the centrality of the proclamation of Scripture in the liturgical assembly. The church is firm in its conviction that every time it reads the Scripture in the liturgy, it is Christ himself who speaks, proclaiming the Good News again.

The purpose of our reflection here is to explain why and how every believer can, in a conscious way, make the church's faith in the word of God his own. We will consider the gospel episode of Jesus reading the Scriptures at Nazareth for insight into the theological meaning and the spiritual value of the church's practice, right from its origins,

6. Second Vatican Council, *Sacrosanctum Concilium*, n. 7.
7. Ibid., n. 33.

of reading the Scriptures of the liturgy. We will consider the Liturgy of the Word in light of two scriptural accounts in which biblical texts are read in liturgical contexts. Jesus' reading of Isaiah in the Nazareth synagogue points us to the scribe Ezra's solemn reading of the book of the Law in Jerusalem (see Neh 8:1-12). Both of these biblical accounts include three basic elements:

1. the community gathered as an assembly
2. the book of the canonical Scriptures
3. the reader proclaiming the passage

These same three constitutive elements are present in the Christian Liturgy of the Word. Within the spiritual dynamic between community, book, and reader is the hearing of the word of God that is contained in the Scriptures, proclaimed by the reader, and heard by the assembly. In every Liturgy of the Word, there is an interaction between community, Scripture, and the voice of the reader, and through this interaction the word of God becomes event, happening in an efficacious way.

Here is the episode of Jesus in the synagogue of Nazareth narrated in Luke 4:16-21:

> When he [Jesus] came to Nazareth, where he had been brought up, he went to the synagogue on the sabbath day, as was his custom. He stood up to read, and the scroll of the prophet Isaiah was given to him. He unrolled the scroll and found the place where it was written:
> "The Spirit of the Lord is upon me,
> because he has anointed me to bring good news to the poor.
> He has sent me to proclaim release to the captives
> and recovery of sight to the blind,
> to let the oppressed go free,
> to proclaim the year of the Lord's favor."

And he rolled up the scroll, gave it back to the attendant, and sat down. The eyes of all in the synagogue were fixed on him. Then he began to say to them, "Today this scripture has been fulfilled in your hearing."

## The Community Rooted in Hearing

Jesus "went to the synagogue on the sabbath day." He did not simply enter this place of worship; he united himself to the community gathered there in liturgical assembly. "[H]e went to the synagogue" describes much more than his physical actions; it means convening together with the believers of the same place (*epì tò autó*: 1 Cor 11:20) in order to be a member of the *qehal Adonaj*, the gathering of the Lord. For a child of Israel to enter a synagogue for the common prayer, for a Christian to enter a church, for every believer to enter his place of worship, means entering into and becoming part of a people's entire history of faith. It means choosing to be a member of the historical body, present and past, of the community of believers.

The *qehal Adonaj*, the people of God gathered in holy assembly, is the end and the image of the entire journey of salvation through which God accompanied Israel: from the condition of servitude to that of service (*'avodà*) offered to God. Worship, service, the adoration of the Lord is the very purpose of the liberation of Israel from slavery in Egypt, according to God's revelation to Moses: "[W]hen you have brought the people out of Egypt, you shall worship God on this mountain" (Exod 3:12). To serve the Lord means to grow progressively into fullest freedom. To adore the Lord means to escape from the slavery of idolatry in order to grow in the exercise of one's freedom. The Lord God of Israel, in fact, can be adored only by a free people. Which god is adored is the demonstration of whether one is still a slave or has become a daughter or son. It is not by chance that for both "Israel . . . my firstborn son" (Exod 4:22; cf. Deut 1:31 and Hos 11:1) and Jesus "my Son, the Beloved" (Luke 3:22), one of the temptations encountered in the desert is the temptation to adore the idol. It is the test of worship. To the tempter, Jesus responded,

> Worship the Lord your God,
> and serve only him. (Luke 4:8)

Here Jesus is, in a sense, repeating in a different way the response he has already given to his parents in the temple of Jerusalem: "Did you not know that I must be in my Father's house?" (Luke 2:49). In the desert, it is as though Jesus rejects the tempter saying, "Don't you know that what fills my heart is not the power and glory of this world, of which I am not a slave, but my Father, whose son I am?"

Jesus knows well that what people are disposed to adore reveals what is in their hearts. He knows that worship is a question not just of rite but of ethos. It is that profound truth that fills the heart of every person and that orients her choices and guides her behavior. For Israel, for Jesus, and for every believer, what we prostrate before, what we adore, reveals the desires we have decided to serve. To those Jews who obstinately opposed his word, Jesus said, "You are from your father the devil, and you choose to do your father's desires" (John 8:44). From the assembly in the desert to the assembly in the synagogue of Nazareth, to become a part of the *qahal Adonaj* means to confess which father we have chosen and to say publicly to who whom we belong: to the Lord and to the community of the children he calls.

The first datum that emerges from Luke's account is therefore the synagogue, which before being the place of Jewish gathering for worship is the very name of the community gathered, called by God, to hear God's word on the day God has made holy. Jesus unites himself to the synagogue by taking part in the sabbath prayer and listening to the readings from the Law and the Prophets. In the same way, the first element of the assembly of Ezra, narrated in Nehemiah 8:1-12, is the calling together of the people who will become the first assembly of Israel after the return from the Babylonian exile, summoned by the governor Nehemiah in order to hear the book of the Law. The account begins in this way:

> Now when the seventh month came, the whole people gathered as one in the square in front of the Water Gate, and they called upon Ezra the scribe to bring forth the book of the law of Moses which the Lord had commanded for Israel. On the first day of the seventh month, therefore, Ezra the priest brought the law before the assembly, which consisted of men, women, and those children old enough to understand. (Neh 8:1-2, NABRE)

In the middle of the fifth century BC, the people of Israel returned from exile had rebuilt the Temple at great effort, and now, with a solemn reading led by Ezra, the expert scribe of the law of Moses (cf. Ezra 7:10), they listen to the Law proclaimed.

The subject of the action is the people of Israel, who make up the holy assembly of the Lord. The suggestive expression "as one" describes more than the simple result of gathering; it speaks of a unanimity of spirit that joins those present. This unanimity is rooted in their being mutually called together, which is often, in the Bible, a characteristic of the assemblies of Israel. The expression "the whole people gathered as one" is also found in the book of Ezra (cf. Ezra 3:1), referring to the assembly called together to build the altar, the work that began the construction of the second Temple. In the same way, the assembly of Sinai, which is the arche-

type of every Israelite assembly, is marked by the concord
and unanimity of the people in response to the word of the
Lord proclaimed by Moses: "[A]ll the people answered with
one voice and said, 'All the words that the LORD has spoken
we will do' " (Exod 24:3; cf. 19:8). This is the nature of the
*qehal Adonaj*: "one [person]," "one voice."

The narrator specifies that the assembly of Ezra is made
up of "men, women, and those children old enough to understand," meaning all of the citizens of Jerusalem who were
at least ten years old, without exception. This indicates the
interest and the oneness of the assembly that is the epiphany
of the entire community of "those who had returned from
the captivity" (Neh 8:17). The experience of the exile is, de-
finitively, what is held in common by the members of this
assembly called to hear the reading of the law of Moses.

The text specifies that the assembly gathered "in the
square in front of the Water Gate," south of the Temple of
Jerusalem. It is an area that was not considered sacred.
What is most surprising is that in this biblical text, which
was written after the second Temple was built and then
consecrated in 515 BC—as narrated in the book of Ezra
(cf. Ezra 4:24ff.)—the assembly does not gather in a sacred
Temple area but in the main square of Jerusalem. This is
significant, since the public squares were the places where
the synagogues arose.

A specific time of the assembly of Ezra is also noted: "the
first day of the seventh month." This is the beginning of
the festival of autumn, during which—beginning from the
fifteenth day of the same month—the feast of booths is
celebrated. It is the most popular and joyful of Israel's
feasts and is therefore called "the festival of the LORD" (Lev
23:39), the feast of feasts. It is important to note that while
Leviticus prescribes for the feast of booths that "[t]he first
day shall be a holy convocation. . . . Seven days you shall

present the Lord's offerings by fire" (Lev 23:35-36), the book of Nehemiah reports instead that "day by day, from the first day to the last day, [Ezra] read from the book of the law of God. They kept the festival seven days; and on the eighth day there was a solemn assembly, according to the ordinance" (Neh 8:18). The reading of the book of the Law is carried out with the same frequency, and therefore assumes the same importance, as the offering of sacrifice in the Temple. The great feast of the return of the exiles to Jerusalem is marked by the hearing of the word of God. To understand the meaning and the import of the reading of the Law over the seven days that preceded the feast of booths in the place of the offering of sacrifice, it is necessary to recall that it was on the occasion of this feast that King Solomon had dedicated the first Temple of Jerusalem, transferring the ark of the covenant to its place there. From that day, the cloud of the glory of the Lord, the Shekhina, the sign of the presence of God among his people, took up its dwelling in the Temple (cf. 1 Kgs 8).

The assembly of Ezra, therefore, has as its background this foundational event in the history of Israel, Solomon's placing in the Temple the ark of the covenant, inside of which "[t]here was nothing . . . except the two tablets of stone that Moses had placed there at Horeb, where the Lord had made a covenant with the Israelites, when they came out of the land of Egypt" (1 Kgs 8:9). Now, on their return from the Babylonian exile, with this public and solemn reading of the book of the law of Moses before all the people, God once again takes up dwelling among the people who hear his word, renewing the covenant with the children of Israel. This is the day "Judaism is born,"[8] the religion of the Torah.

---

8. This is the title given by *The Jerusalem Bible* to the eighth chapter of the book of Nehemiah (*The Jerusalem Bible* [Garden City, NY: Doubleday, 1966], 589).

The first element that emerges from both biblical accounts we have considered here is the community of believers gathered in liturgical assembly. This is the primary narrative datum, because it is the primary theological datum—and therefore the primary liturgical datum as well. The community precedes the Scriptures because before the Bible, there was the people of the Bible. Theologically and chronologically, the experience of faith of the believers, who recognized and confessed the salvific work of God, came first, and then came the Scriptures. The believing community that professes its faith in God and God's saving work both precedes and is foundational to the book of the Scriptures. The events initiated by God that the believing community recognized as saving events on their behalf were first. This recognition is a confession of faith, and this confession is in itself a celebration of faith; it is a liturgical act. This liturgical confession of faith becomes written testimony, instituted permanently in time and space, and is therefore normative for the community that recognizes in it the word of God, the norm of its faith. It is because the faith of the community that confesses and celebrates the salvific works of God precedes the holy Scriptures that the liturgical assembly is the fundamental hermeneutical setting of the Scriptures: they are heard and understood fully in the *ekklesía* because they were born in the liturgical assembly.

More eloquent than any discourse, in this regard, is the liturgical norm that is still in force today in the synagogue worship (and analogously in Christian worship), according to which the scroll of the Law cannot be taken from the ark (*aron*) and read if there are not present at least ten adult men (*minjan*). This norm suggests above all that it is not enough for the book of the Law to be present and that someone reads from it; also necessary is people to hear it proclaimed. This is the essential and decisive difference between the personal study of biblical texts and the liturgical proclamation of the Scriptures. There can be no direct and individual relationship with the Scriptures, for between the book and the individual listener there is the *qehal Adonaj*, the *ekklesía*, the liturgical community of believers. The book, the one who reads it, and the one who hears it must each always be understood within the context of the *ekklesía*. Hearing the Scriptures happens fully and authentically only within the church, because that is where the Scriptures were born. There are not Scriptures and also tradition; there is only the Scriptures within tradition.

## The Book of the Scriptures

The second element of the Liturgy of the Word is the book of the Scriptures. Luke narrates: "[Jesus] stood up to read, and the scroll of the prophet was given to him. He unrolled the scroll" (Luke 4:16-17). It is a scroll, not a book, but what is decisive is that it is a written text. Jesus, standing, takes in his hands the scroll of the prophet—this is a symbol, the same one to which the high priest Jonathan refers in First Maccabees when he describes the children of Israel: "we have as encouragement the holy books that are in our hands" (1 Macc 12:9). The Christ who takes in his hands the scroll of the Scriptures is a true and proper Christological icon, an image that is for Ivan Illich unique and important:

> Not a single pre-Christian god of Mediterranean antiquity has a book or a scroll in his hands. In this, Christ is unique. He alone has divine attributes, *and* wields a scroll. He both *is* the word and *reveals* the book. The Word becomes Flesh in the Book. Writing becomes an allegory for the Incarnation in the Womb of the Virgin. Hence the liturgical reverence for the book as object.[9]

9. Ivan Illich, *In the Vineyard of the Text: A Commentary to Hugh's Didascalicon* (Chicago: University of Chicago Press, 1993), 122.

As called for by the synagogue rite, the scroll is handed to the lector Jesus so that he may read it before the community. The attendant puts it into his hands because it is not the property of the lector. That is also why we see that Jesus, on finishing the reading, "rolled up the scroll [and] gave it back to the attendant" (Luke 4:20). The scroll is not his but the community's. He has received it from the community and he returns it to the community. The community is its authorized caretaker. Similarly, in the Christian liturgical assembly, the lector receives from the church the book of canonical texts to read. It is not the lector's but the church's. By placing it on the ambo, the church puts it into the lector's hands. On finishing the reading, the lector does not carry the book away but leaves it with the assembly, because it is in the assembly's care, just as the Eucharist is.

In an identical way, we read in the book of Nehemiah:

> Now when the seventh month came, the whole people gathered as one in the square in front of the Water Gate, and they called upon Ezra the scribe to bring forth the book of the law of Moses which the LORD had commanded for Israel. On the first day of the seventh month, therefore, Ezra the priest brought the law before the assembly, which consisted of men, women, and those children old enough to understand. In the square in front of the Water Gate, Ezra read out of the book from daybreak till midday, in the presence of the men, the women, and those children old enough to understand; and all the people listened attentively to the book of the law. (Neh 8:1-2, NABRE)

What is described here is a true and proper liturgy of the book of the law of Moses, which is in its substance the Torah: "the whole people gathered as one . . . and they called upon Ezra the scribe to bring forth the book of the law of Moses." It is essential to note that it is the assembly that calls upon Ezra to bring forth the book of the Law, almost invoking its presence. In this way, the people who are gathered there together show that they are aware of truly being the holy assembly, before which must be the word that the Lord has addressed to them. "Ezra the priest brought the law before the assembly": here the book of the Law is before the assembly and the assembly is before the book of the Law, expressing clearly the reciprocal presence of the Lord and his people. The covenant partners stand before one another. The Lord addresses his word and the people hear it.

The scribe Ezra who brings the book of the Law before the assembly and the attendant who hands the scroll of Isaiah to Jesus both carry out the same liturgical action. With gestures and words, both express the reciprocal belonging between the community and the Scriptures. The assembly that calls for the book of the Law and the open hands of Jesus in the act of receiving the scroll of the prophet—both are instances of texts placed before the eyes and in the hands, because in the texts the community recognizes its own identity and Jesus finds what is written of himself. The norm, then, is not the book itself but the book before the eyes and in the hands of the community. This explains why the book cannot be without the community, cannot be isolated from the community. The *ekklesía*, the liturgical assembly, demonstrates the impossibility of *sola Scriptura*.

Let us note, finally, a last bit of data, simple but significant. As called for by the synagogue liturgy in Jesus' time, Jesus received from the community not only the scroll of Isaiah but also the specific passage he was to read. He read the *haftarà*, the passage called for by the synagogue lectionary on the sabbath following the reading of the *parashà*, a passage of the Torah. In the same way, when the lector in the Christian liturgy receives from the church the book of biblical passages (the lectionary), he may not choose whatever passage he likes most; rather, he must read the passage assigned by the church in the lectionary for that day.

## The Necessary Visibility of the Word

One important element worth our consideration is the rituality connected to the book in the context of the community. The account of the assembly of Ezra in Nehemiah illustrates the importance of the visibility of the book of the law of the Lord:

> Ezra brought the law before the assembly. . . . The scribe Ezra stood on a wooden platform that had been made for the purpose. . . . Ezra opened the book in the sight of all the people, for he was standing above all the people; and when he opened it, all the people stood up. Then Ezra blessed the Lord, the great God, and all the people answered, "Amen, Amen," lifting up their hands. Then they bowed their heads and worshiped the Lord with their faces to the ground. (Neh 8:2, 4-6)

These are liturgical words and gestures of special intensity: the book of the Law must be seen before it is heard, because it has a necessary visibility. The scroll of the Law is held up before the eyes of the people, who stand to express their respect and veneration. The scribe Ezra offered a benediction, and the assembly responds with a double "Amen," a confession of faith, along with gestures that express fear, adoration, and respect. With all of these, the people express their faith: to be before the book of the Law is to be before the Lord.

Lifting the scroll of the Torah before the eyes of all is, then, a ritual action that manifests the holy presence of

God in the midst of his people. Still today, the rite of *hag-bahà* ("raising up") remains a part of the Sephardic synagogue liturgy: before the reading, the scroll of the Law is removed from the ark and the minister (not necessarily the lector) holds it open on his arms facing the community in a gesture of elevation and exposition. He then passes through the synagogue before all the people, while they venerate it and kiss it, singing, "This is the law that Moses set before the Israelites" (Deut 4:44) and "at the command of the LORD by Moses" (Num 9:23). According to the Talmud, to lead the *hagbahà* is more honorable even than to be called to read the Law before the assembly.[10] In the Ashkenazi liturgy, this rite is called the *ghelità* ("rolling up"), and it comes instead at the end of the reading from the Torah and before the reading from the Prophets. Finally, in some Hassidic synagogues the *hagbahà* happens both before and after the Torah reading.

Certainly analogous to the *hagbahà* in the Christian liturgy is the elevation of the Evangelarium. This action demonstrates to us that in the liturgy the book of God's word is presented before the eyes of the assembly before it is heard as text that is read to the assembly. The elevation of the Scriptures before the eyes of the people is already, in itself, a hermeneutic action. Besides the words of the homily, liturgical gestures also carry out a hermeneutical function. Before being read and heard, the book is seen. In the liturgy, before one hears the word of God, one sees the book that contains it. The church presents to the faithful gathered in assembly the sign of their identity; the Evangelarium therefore has a triple symbolic function. First, elevating it before the eyes of the people, the church recalls the superiority and authority of the word of God over every human

10. Cf. b*Meghilla* 32a, in Lazarus Goldschmidt, ed., *Der babilonische Talmud* IV (Konigstein: Judischer Verlag, 1980), 131.

word. Second, the church declares that the book is shown to all because it belongs to all, and that all have free access to the word of salvation. Third, the church witnesses to the reality that this singular word of salvation creates a relationship among the believers who gather, for they recognize themselves as participants in a unique covenant.

For André Fossion the book of the Scriptures and the assembly represent the two halves of a *sýmbolon* cut in two, one piece given to each partner of a covenant. Bringing back together the two parts of the *sýmbolon*—Scriptures and assembly, representing God and the people —is the way that covenant partners confirm and renew their covenant.

> Holding the book in view, opening it, reading it before the assembly are each gestures that ritualize the covenant. The Scriptures are the efficacious sign with which Christians can recognize themselves as participants in a covenant in the name of the God of Jesus Christ. They proclaim their common belonging and their differentiation from other human communities. Consequently, the Scriptures are inseparable from the social relationships that they establish. The book constitutes the people; the corpus of biblical texts constitute the bonds of the ecclesial body, the proper functioning of which is guaranteed by the continually repeated reading of the Scriptures.[11]

Paraphrasing the well-known adage of patristic inspiration formulated by Henri de Lubac, according to which "the church produces the Eucharist, but the Eucharist also produces the church,"[12] we can say without hesitation that

11. A. Fossion, *Leggere le Scritture. Teoria e pratica della lettura strutturale* (Leumann: Elledice, 1982), 52.

12. Henri de Lubac, *The Splendor of the Church* (San Francisco: Ignatius Press, 1999), 133.

it is also true that "the church makes the Scriptures and the Scriptures make the church."

The elevation of the book so that the entire assembly can see the Scriptures is therefore the first act of the liturgy carried out in the assembly of Ezra. The Christian liturgy, too, in its most solemn form, includes two elevations of the Evangelarium. The first is during the initial procession, when the deacon carries it high through the midst of the assembly, finally placing it on the altar, where it rests until the proclamation of the gospel reading. This placing of the Book of the Gospels upon the altar demonstrates well that the altar is—even before the ambo—the primary place of the liturgy. The second elevation of the Evangelarium comes during the procession when the deacon brings the book from the altar to the ambo for the reading.

It is clear by now that many ritual elements common to all Christian liturgy correspond to the gestures of veneration of the book of the law of God that are narrated in Nehemiah and that are present also in the various ritual synagogue traditions that we have cited above. However, there is one principle element of the liturgical reading of the Scriptures that points ritually to the irreducible difference between Christian and Jewish theologies of the Word of God. In synagogue worship, the scroll of the Law is taken from the *aron* in which it is always stored, while the church's liturgy, the Evangelarium is taken from the altar after being placed there at the beginning of the celebration.

## Evangelarium and Altar, "Word of the Cross" and Eucharist

By placing the Evangelarium at the center of the altar at the beginning of the liturgy, when the altar is free of any other object, the church recognizes in the Book of the Gospels the same dignity possessed by the eucharistic gifts. On the altar, the Evangelarium has the place of the Eucharist. It is not only an object used *in* worship. It is an object *of* worship. Placing the Evangelarium on the altar is a liturgical act that expresses an intensely theological idea taught by the Second Vatican Council: the Christian is nourished by "the bread of life . . . from the one table of the Word of God and the Body of Christ."[13] We should recall that in the Eastern churches, the Book of the Gospels is enthroned on the altar even outside of liturgical celebrations.

What mystery of faith is expressed in the act of taking the Evangelarium from the altar? Just as the eucharistic bread and wine are taken from the altar so that the faithful may nourish themselves on the body of Christ, so also the gospel is taken from the altar so that the faithful may be nourished with the word of Christ. In the Fourth Gospel, Jesus says not only that "[t]hose who eat my flesh and drink my blood have eternal life" (John 6:54) but also that "anyone who hears my word . . . has eternal life" (John 5:24). The Evangelarium is taken from the altar in order to witness to the community's hearing and eucharistic consuming of the Word of God. And so in the *Rationale divinorum officiorum*, William Durandus (d. 1296) interprets the meaning of the deacon taking the Evangelarium from the altar: "The reason the book is taken from the altar is that the apostles received the Gospel from the altar when, in their preaching, they announced the passion of the Lord."[14]

For Durandus, the apostles "received the Gospel from the altar"—the altar, almost personified, is the one who gives the book—because the preaching of the gospel is

---

13. Second Vatican Council, *Dei Verbum*, n. 21.

14. Guillaume Durand, *Rationale divinorum officiorum* IV, 24, 5, ed. A. Davril and T.M. Thibodeau (Turnholti: Brepols, 1995), 343.

always and before all else the proclamation of the passion of Christ. We can therefore observe that at the beginning of the liturgy the Evangelarium is placed on the altar, the place of the memorial of the sacrifice of the cross, and then taken from there for the proclamation of the gospel from the ambo, meaning that the Gospel of Christ must be heard in the context of the mystery of the cross, because the preaching of the gospel is always the preaching of "the message about the cross" (1 Cor 1:18). "[W]e proclaim Christ crucified" (1 Cor 1:23), Paul confesses. So the lifting up and the enthronement of the Evangelarium before the eyes of the assembly is already a proclamation of the *verbum crucis*. It is as though the one who carries out this action says silently to the people, "Ecce verbum crucis," echoing the ancient song *Ecce lignum crucis*, which the celebrant intones three times while elevating the cross at the solemn Good Friday liturgy. Elevating the cross and elevating the Evangelarium are the same act, and it proclaims the same Word, the Word of the cross.

That the gospel and the cross are inseparable is attested also by the small sign of the cross that the one who proclaims the gospel traces on the page of the Evangelarium, a gesture that he then repeats together with the faithful on his forehead, his lips, and his chest, signifying their openness to the Word of the gospel in their most basic faculties: intellect, speech, and will. A memorial of the baptismal *sphragís*, this gesture represents a cruciform incision of the *verbum crucis* on the forehead, the place of one's mind and intelligence; on the lips, the place of one's voice and the words one speaks; and on the heart, the place of one's will and emotions. The meaning of this sign of the cross traced first by the deacon on the gospel page and then by all the faithful three times on themselves brings William Durandus to call the Evangelarium the *liber Crucifixi*: "This is the book or the Gospel of God. This is the book of the

Crucified One [*liber Crucifixi*] that I preach. This is the book of the man of peace from whom we have received reconciliation, as the Apostles says: 'We preach Christ crucified.'"[15]

An effective synthesis of the connection between the Evangelarium and the altar, and therefore between the Word of the cross and the Eucharist, is offered by Augustine in one of those incisive expressions of which he was a master: "We . . . are fed from the Lord's cross . . . when we eat his body."[16]

Even at the heart of the eucharistic celebration, at the moment the faithful receive the body and blood of the Lord, the liturgy reminds us of the intimate relationship between the Book of the Gospels and the altar, between the Word and the Eucharist. A synthesis of this entire liturgical dynamic is the communion antiphon. It is all that remains today of the ancient communion chant called the *Communio*. When, from the thirteenth century, the reception of communion by the faithful disappeared and with it the need for the communion chant, only this antiphon remained, retaining the significant name *Communio*. A fragment of what it once was and so miniscule as to be habitually ignored, the communion antiphon reminds us that the Catholic Church in its liturgy has never forgotten the connection between the *manducatio panis* and the *manducatio verbi*, even when theological reflection forgot.[17] The communion antiphon is a brief biblical verse that can be read aloud by the lector or celebrant before the distribution of

15. Ibid., IV, 24, 26, p. 217.

16. Augustine, *Expositions of the Psalms*, vol. 5, trans. Maria Boulding (Hyde Park, NY: New City Press, 2003), 40.

17. Cf. Marie-Philippe Schüermans, *Parole de Dieu et rite sacramental. Étude critique des antiennes de communion néotestamnetaires* (Brussels: Lumen Vitae, 1963).

communion. This fragment of the word of God is proclaimed, so to speak, "over" the eucharistic bread and chalice, so that the broken Word and the broken bread form a
single reality, the sacrament of the same mystery.

Hearing a passage from the gospel just proclaimed before receiving communion reinforces the unity of the table
of Christ, the bread of life who nourishes believers with
his scriptural body and his eucharistic body. We our nourished, at the same time, with the piece of bread and the
word of the Lord; by communicating in the bread, the
faithful also communicate in the Word. The fragment of
bread takes on, so to speak, the flavor of the gospel. In the
eucharistic celebration, then, there are not two commu-
nions—one in the word of the Lord and one in the body of
the Lord. Rather, communion in the holy gifts is in itself
communion in the holy gospel; the Eucharist is the body
of the Word. In the liturgy, the hearing of the word of God
contained in the Scriptures does not end when the last
verse of the gospel reading is proclaimed; it continues to
be heard in different ways throughout the eucharistic celebration.

Also significant is the fact that the communion antiphon
is proclaimed just prior to the distribution of the Eucharist
to the faithful. Preceding communion, the gospel verse
becomes an invitation. The same word of God that has
called the believer into his presence now invites the believer into communion with God, to be nourished at the
table of the bread of life and to drink from the chalice of
salvation: "Wisdom has mixed her wine, she has also set
her table, and proclaimed, 'Come, eat of my bread, and
drink of the wine I have mixed'" (see Prov 9:1-5). But the
communion antiphon proclaimed before receiving the
Eucharist is also an appeal, almost an admonition addressed to the faithful: do not nourish yourselves on the
eucharistic body of the Lord if you have not heard, ac-

cepted, and obeyed his word. There can be no true *manducatio panis* without a *manducatio verbi*.

But the most important and decisive meaning of the communion antiphon is its insistence that for the Christian, the word of salvation heard in the gospel reading proclaimed in a liturgy is fully realized only through the communion in the body and blood of Christ that follows it. The proclamation of the Scriptures in the liturgy reaches its summit in communion in the body and blood of Christ. The Evangelarium is placed on the altar at the beginning of the liturgy because the altar on which the bread is broken is the *télos*, the destination point of the gospel that has been heard; believers are fully obedient to the word of God only by their communion in the sacrifice of the altar, in the freedom Christ has won by offering his life for the salvation of the world. It is in the breaking of the bread, then, that the Word that is heard is fully revealed. Gregory the Great expressed this with spiritual wisdom when he wrote, regarding the story of the disciples on the road to Emmaus, "They . . . recognized in the breaking of the bread the God they did not know as he explained the sacred scriptures."[18]

## The Voice of the Lector

Jesus, we read in Luke's account, "unrolled the scroll and found the place where it was written: 'The Spirit of the Lord is upon me . . .'" (Luke 4:17-18). Let us consider the act of opening the book of the Scriptures (or opening the scroll), an act that is itself a liturgy. "The iconic significance of the book and the mystagogical power of opening and closing it

18. Gregory the Great, *Forty Gospel Homilies*, trans. Dom Hurst (Piscataway, NJ: Gorgias Press, 2009), 177.

cannot be denied."[19] This is why the liturgy of the opening
of the book of the Scriptures is solemnized in the book of
the Scriptures itself. It is carried out by the scribe Ezra, who
"opened the book in the sight of the people . . . and when
he opened it, all the people stood up" (Neh 8:5); it is done
by Jesus in the synagogue of Nazareth; and it is also performed by the Lamb in the liturgy of heaven: "Who is worthy to open the scroll and break its seals?" (Rev 5:2), the
mighty angel proclaims with a loud voice, and when the
Lamb takes the book "from the right hand of the one who
was seated on the throne" (Rev 5:7), the heavenly creatures
and elders sing out: "You are worthy to take the scroll and
open its seals" (Rev 5:9). Opening the book is therefore the
eschatological act performed in the liturgy of heaven by the
slain Lamb. It is an act that reveals the mystery. And so
François Cassingena-Trévedy reflects on the moment that
Jesus opens the scroll of Isaiah:

> It is a fascinating scene, a unique moment in which the
> One who is proclaimed makes the proclamation, the
> Meaning of the text takes the text in his very hands, and
> the Exegete (cf. John 1:18: *exeghésato*) offers an exegesis
> of his own word.[20]

In the synagogue of Nazareth, Jesus the exegete "unrolled the scroll" and "rolled up the scroll" (Luke 4:17, 20).
Gilbert of Hoyland, one of the most astute of the Cistercian
fathers, saw in these two gestures an image of *lectio divina*
and, by extension, the exegetical task:

19. J.-Y. Hameline, "Le site cérémoniel du livre," in *Chroniques
d'art sacré* 67 (2001): 23.

20. F. Cassingena-Trévedy, *Nazareth, maison du livre. Nouvelles
considérations sur la Lectio divina* (Geneva: Ad Solem, 2004), 50.

Hold fast what you hold, hold and touch lingeringly and lovingly the word of life. Unroll the scroll of life, the scroll which Jesus unrolls or, rather, which is Jesus. Wrap yourself in him. . . . Put on your Beloved, our Lord Jesus Christ. . . . [H]is word is a flame.[21]

We must not miss the fact that it was specifically at the *beginning* of his ministry that Jesus entered the Nazareth synagogue and "unrolled the scroll." His taking and opening the prophetic scroll is, as we have noted, the first gesture of his ministry, just as his taking and "opening" the bread at the Last Supper was the final gesture of his ministry.[22] From the alpha to the omega of his ministry, Jesus carries out the same act, the same liturgy: he takes the scroll and he takes his own body and, taking it in his hands, the scroll becomes his scriptural body, his body given, handed over, offered. He is written about in the scroll of the prophet, just as his mystery is inscribed in the broken bread.

Taking the book and opening it: only the Lamb and no one else is worthy to carry out this act because he was slain (cf. Rev 5:9). The Lamb of Revelation carries out the very same gesture that Jesus did in the Nazareth synagogue: he receives the book and opens it in order to reveal his mystery. Bernard of Clairvaux writes, "Worthy is the Lamb that was slain, the lion that rose from the dead, and finally, the book worthy to open itself."[23] And Hugh of St. Victor

---

21. Gilbert of Hoyland, *Sermons on the Song of Songs*, vol. 1, trans. Lawrence C. Braceland (Kalamazoo, MI: Cistercian Publications, 1978), 14: 1, 166.

22. Cf. Cassingena-Trévedy, *Nazareth*, 51.

23. Bernard of Clairvaux, "On the Resurrection of the Lord, Sermon 1," in *Sermons for Lent and the Easter Season*, ed. John Leinenweber and Mark Scott (Collegeville, MN: Liturgical Press, Cistercian Publications, 2013), 143.

comments, "All of Scripture is one book and this book is Christ, because all of Scripture speaks of Christ and finds its fulfillment in Christ."[24]

Consider, then, Jesus the lector who reads the prophecy, "The Spirit of the Lord is upon me." In this, the only passage of all the gospels in which Scripture is read aloud, Jesus reads a single verse—Isaiah 6:1—to demonstrate that every verse of Scripture discloses the mystery of Christ. It is a single verse, and it speaks of him, the *Verbum abbreviatum*, as the ancient and medieval fathers called him. *Verbum abbreviatum et abbrevians* ("the shortened and shortening word") and *salubre compendium* ("synthesis of salvation"), as Bernard describes him.[25] Consider Jesus the lector who is always inseparable from the book. This lector is one with what is written, because Scripture is written to be proclaimed.

But here Jesus is standing and reading aloud. The voice of the lector—we cannot emphasize enough the importance, the necessity, of the voice. In the lector's voice, the book that contains the word of God is handed over to the community. The Scripture in which the community recognizes itself must be proclaimed. It needs a voice. While every book's readers are in some way inscribed in the book itself, the Scriptures bear not only those who read it but the voice of the lector. In Hebrew, as we have noted, the Scriptures are *miqra'*, which means "read aloud," permanently linking the Scriptures and the need for them to be read aloud. The word *miqra'* derives from the root *q r'e* and from the verb *qara'*, "to read aloud, to call out, to cry

---

24. Hugh of Saint-Victor, *De Arca Noe Morali*, 2, 8. [My translation from the Italian.—Trans.]

25. Bernard of Clairvaux, *On Loving God*, VII, 21, trans. Emero Stiegman (Kalamazoo, MI: Cistercian Publications, 1973, 1995), 23.

out"—all verbs linked to hearing. Therefore, in Hebrew, to say "Scripture" is to say at the same time "Proclaimed," that which is intended to be read aloud and heard. The liturgical reading of the Scriptures accomplish the transition, essential to the Scriptures themselves, from written word to oral proclamation.

The voice of the lector belongs, then, in a constitutive way to the text, and it is the lector's task to ensure that her voice serves the "written voice," as Paul Ricoeur has called it, the demand, written into the text, that the text speaks to and challenges those who hear it:

> It is not a vocal voice, so to speak, released from the body upon the breath. There is, in scripture, an analog of the voice, *a written voice*. It is a voice without a mouth, without a face or expression, a voice without a body. And yet it is a voice that challenges the lector, *the equivalent* of the connection that the spoken voice has with the word. In the rare moment of blessed reading, one can truly say that reading is not to be seen but to be heard.[26]

What does the voice of the lector do? The voice relies on what is written, never taking the place of the Scripture itself. The voice submits itself to what is written, as Jesus submitted himself to what was written by Isaiah. Jesus, the eternal Word of the Father, did not invent a text but, obeying what was written, gave obedience to Moses and Elijah, to the Law and the Prophets, and in doing so gave obedience to the Father.

If the Scripture keeps the voice from occupying the place of the author, God, it is also important to understand at the same time that the voice attests that what is written is

---

26. Paul Ricoeur, "Éloge de la lecture et de l'écriture," *Études théologiques et religieuses* 64 (1989): 405 (italics mine).

not enough, the text must return to be word. The lector's voice that is heard in the midst of the community makes clear the need for the process of reading, of hearing, of interpretation and actualization, without which the Bible would be nothing but a dead letter.

Behold, then, what the celebration of the Word, the liturgy of reading, produces: the voice submitting itself to what is written brings the written word alive. It resuscitates the otherwise dead letter of the Bible, the door to life. This led Ivan Illich to observe, "Reading the man-made book is an act of midwifery. Reading, far from being an act of abstraction, is an act of incarnation."[27] For this reason, to proclaim the Scripture before the community means more than simply reading it aloud; it means speaking the Word of life to the community in the name of the Lord. The Scripture becomes the word addressed, the word proclaimed, the creator of community. In the Liturgy of the Word, through the Scriptures, God speaks and this speech forms, shapes, creates the community. This is an event that only the word of the Lord can accomplish.[28] In this sense, as the council affirms in a passage already cited above, "in the liturgy God speaks to his people, and Christ is still proclaiming his Gospel."[29] This explains the reason that the assembly acclaims, at the end of the proclamation of the gospel: "Praise to you, Lord Jesus Christ." The liturgy puts on the lips of the assembly a great profession of faith, so that "this 'to you' . . . conveys the assembly's act of faith in the nature of that which has just happened, or

27. Illich, *In the Vineyard of the Text*, 123.
28. Cf. Enzo Bianchi, *La Parola costruisce la comunità* (Bose: Qiqajon, 1993).
29. Second Vatican Council, *Sacrosanctum Concilium*, n. 33.

better, in the one who has spoken to us."[30] In this case, it is not someone speaking *in persona Christi*, but rather *Christus in persona* speaks to his community so that the church may hear him and actualize in itself his word. *"Os Christi, evangelium est"* is how Augustine admirably summarized this idea: "The Gospel is the mouth of Christ."[31]

"He stood up to read," Luke writes, telling of Jesus' carrying out the liturgical ministry of lector on that Sabbath day in Nazareth. We are not told whether Jesus knew in advance that he would be reading the scroll of the prophet before the community or if he was prepared to do it; we do know, from the teaching of the rabbis, the expectation that the one who carries out this ministry should do it with dignity and seriousness, as respect for the Word of God would demand. In the rabbinical texts, the lector is exhorted to stand up straight, to speak loudly and clearly, to pronounce the words carefully, to dress in a dignified way, and on the previous evening to prepare carefully by reading the passage several times.[32] In one passage, Rabbi Aqiba, writing after the destruction of the second temple, admonished synagogue lectors:

> One day the synagogue attendant called upon Rabbi Aqiba to read publicly from the Torah before the community. But he did not want to get up to do the reading. His disciples said, "Teacher, have you not taught us that the Torah is your very life throughout your days? Why are

30. Paul De Clerck, "Un ambon: pourquoi?" *Chroniques d'art sacré* 85 (2006): 8.

31. St. Augustine, Sermon 85.1, in *Sermons*, part 3, vol. 3, trans. Edmund Hill (Brooklyn: New City Press), 391.

32. Cf. H. L. Strack and P. Billerbeck eds., *Kommentar zum Neuen Testament aus Talmud und Midrasch*, vol. 4, bk. 1 (Munich: Beck, 1979), 159.

you refusing to carry out the request?" He told them, "For the temple worship! I have refused to read only because I wasn't able to read the passage several times before-hand, and so I was not prepared. A man, in fact, does not have the right to proclaim the words of the Torah before the community if he has not first repeated them to himself two or three times; God himself acts in this way . . . and before him the Torah is clear as the light of the stars. While he was on the point of entrusting the Torah to the children of Israel, as we read in the book of Job 28:27, "[H]e saw it and declared it; he established it and searched it out"; and only then "he said to humankind" (v. 28).[33]

Following upon rabbinical teaching, the Christian tradition also insists on careful attention to the quality of liturgical reading. Among many possible examples, it is enough for us to recall here the admonition contained in the Rule of Saint Benedict: "[N]o one shall presume to read or sing unless he is able to benefit the hearers; let this be done with humility, seriousness, and reverence, and at the abbot's bidding."[34]

## *The Word of God for the Community*

Luke concludes his story of Jesus in the Nazareth synagogue by saying, "And he rolled up the scroll, gave it back to the attendant, and sat down. The eyes of all in the synagogue were fixed on him. Then he began to say to them, 'Today this scripture has been fulfilled in your hearing.' "

First Jesus "rolled up the scroll." The intelligent and impassioned preacher Ernesto Balducci sees in this gesture an expression of the absolute novelty of Christ's revelation:

---

33. Ibid., 158.
34. *The Rule of St. Benedict* 47, 3–4 (Collegeville, MN: Liturgical Press, 1981), 249.

The scene of Jesus reading the liberation passage from the prophet Isaiah and then rolling up the scroll, while the eyes of everyone in the synagogue are fixed on him, stands in my imagination as the emblem of the absolute novelty of the revelation of Jesus, who is not a man of the book, but who rolled it up. He did not come to ask us to obey written pages—even the pages of the gospels—but to announce, as all eyes are fixed on him, that the prophecy of liberation "today" is fulfilled. . . . Jesus read from the book, but he rolls it up and presents himself as its fulfillment, as the one in whom the time of God is manifested, the Lord's year of grace, the today of God. This shift from the book to the person is fundamental even for us to submit ourselves to its judgment.[35]

The scroll is rolled up, and all eyes in the synagogue are on Jesus. "Then he began to say to them, 'Today this scripture has been fulfilled in your hearing.'" Jesus truly begins to speak when he interprets the Scriptures, and he speaks his first word when the prophecy is fulfilled. The Greek text of this verse is more intense than we typically read it: "Today this Scripture is fulfilled *in your ears*" (*en toîs osìn hymôn*; *in auribus vestris*). In the ears of those who hear it, God fulfills the Scripture proclaimed by Christ. The fulfillment of the Scripture does not happen after it is read but in the very moment it is proclaimed by the lector and heard by those present. For this reason, the opening and the fulfillment of the prophetic text are rooted in the capacity of the listener to hear, to open ears that once were closed. "The eyes of all in the synagogue were fixed on him," but their ears remained closed to him, to the word of revelation proclaimed by Jesus.

35. Ernesto Balducci, *Il tempo di Dio. Ultime omilie* (Fiesole: Cultura della Pace, 1996), 98–99.

If the prophecy of Isaiah that Jesus read announces the liberation of prisoners, we can say that the first prisoner to be freed is the meaning of the text.[36] Jesus does not annul the meaning of the text. He does not render the prophecy surpassed or outdated but present and actualized for the today of those who hear it. "Today this scripture has been fulfilled in your hearing." These few words spoken by Jesus after reading the Isaiah passage contain the essential elements of every spiritual and homiletic commentary on the Scriptures: "today" and not yesterday or tomorrow, the "Scripture" and nothing else; "this Scripture" and not some other passage; "in your hearing" and "for you," precisely for those who are gathered present and for no one else. While he proclaims the Word, Jesus reads it as though it were addressed to himself, because what refers to the prophet will be carried out in his ministry. This is the sole fulfillment of the Scriptures that is possible, the fulfillment above all for himself, of which the psalmist is certain: "The LORD will fulfill his purpose for me" (Ps 138:8).

Origen's well-known comment on this passage from the Gospel of Luke offers the most adequate conclusion of our reflections here, because he suggests the ultimate significance of the reading of the Scriptures in the liturgy:

> "The eyes of all in the synagogue were fixed on him." Now too, if you want it, your eyes can be fixed on the Savior in this synagogue, here in this assembly. For, when you direct the principal power of seeing in your heart to wisdom and truth, and to contemplating God's Only-Begotten, your eyes gaze on Jesus. Blessed is that congregation of which Scripture testifies that "the eyes of all were fixed on him"![37]

---

36. Cf. Cassingena-Trévedy, *Nazareth*, 51.

37. Origen, Homily 32.6, in *Homilies on Luke*, trans. Joseph T. Lienhard (Washington, DC: Catholic University of America Press, 1996), 132–33.

# Chapter Four

# Mystagogy of
# the Presentation of the Gifts

*"Within yourself are the offerings you must present in
praise of God."*

—Augustine of Hippo[1]

Referring to the liturgy's presentation of the gifts, the
*General Instruction for the Roman Missal* (GIRM) observes
realistically, "Even though the faithful no longer bring from
their own possessions the bread and wine intended for the
liturgy as was once the case, nevertheless the rite of carrying up the offerings still keeps its spiritual efficacy and
significance."[2] Though the physical act of bringing the gifts
from home rarely happens today, the spiritual meaning of
bringing the bread and wine to the altar remains intact.
My intent here, therefore, will be to draw out the *vis* and

---

1. St. Augustine, "Exposition of Psalm 55," in *Expositions of the
Psalms 51–72*, trans. Maria Boulding (Hyde Park, NY: New City
Press, 2001), 99.
2. *General Instruction for the Roman Missal*, n. 73, in *The Roman
Missal, Third Edition* (Collegeville, MN: Liturgical Press, 2011), 35.

the *significatio spiritualis*—the efficacy, the power, and the spiritual meaning of this rite.

Since the Eucharist is, as we believe, the source of Christian ethics, I would like to reflect on the rite of the presentation of the gifts first of all as a model and paradigm of such ethics. Inasmuch as it is a eucharistic ethic, it is one of communion with God and of sharing with others, particularly the poor who lack both bread and dignity. The purpose of this chapter is essentially to provide an answer to a single question: *What vision of Christian community, of human community, and therefore of society and the world, emerges from the rite of the presentation of the gifts?* The bringing of the gifts to the altar is a ritual gesture, first Jewish and later Christian, in which three elements interact simultaneously and never independently: the faithful who offer, the gifts that are placed on the altar of the Lord, and the poor with whom the goods of creation are shared.

We will first consider the biblical roots of the ethical duty of the presentation of gifts. It is a duty that Jesus radicalized in the gospels and that the Christian liturgy has integrally made its own. Then we will consider the rite of the presentation of the gifts as we celebrate it today, taking particular note of the blessing of the bread and wine. Finally, we will consider the rite as a call to ethical responsibility.

## The Ethical Command of the Offering of the Firstfruits

Exegetes have made clear that in the ancient text of Deuteronomy 26, the ritual gesture of the offering of the firstfruits is, at the same time, a memorial of the history of Israel, a confession of faith in the action of God, and an ethical command for daily living. In this passage's context,

Israel is a sedentary people, situated in the land of Canaan, and every year, following the harvest, every son of Israel must go up to the sanctuary to bring an offering of the firstfruits of his harvest and to thank the Lord. Moses thus prescribes in the future perfect tense:

> When you have come into the land that the LORD your God is giving you as an inheritance to possess, and you possess it, and settle in it, you shall take some of the first of all the fruit of the ground, which you harvest from the land that the LORD your God is giving you, and you shall put it in a basket and go to the place that the LORD your God will choose as a dwelling for his name. You shall go to the priest who is in office at that time, and say to him, "Today I declare to the LORD your God that I have come in to the land that the LORD swore to our ancestors to give us." When the priest takes the basket from your hand and sets it down before the altar of the LORD your God, you shall make this response before the LORD your God: "A wandering Aramean was my ancestor; he went down into Egypt and lived there as an alien, few in number, and there he became a great nation, mighty and populous. When the Egyptians treated us harshly and afflicted us, by imposing hard labor on us, we cried to the LORD, the God of our ancestors; the LORD heard our voice and saw our affliction, our toil, and our oppression. The LORD brought us out of Egypt with a mighty hand and an outstretched arm, with a terrifying display of power, and with signs and wonders; and he brought us into this place and gave us this land, a land flowing with milk and honey. So now I bring the first of the fruit of the ground that you, O LORD, have given me." You shall set it down before the LORD your God and bow down before the LORD your God. Then you, together with the Levites and the aliens who reside among you, shall celebrate with all the bounty that the LORD your God has given to you and to your house." (Deut 26:1-11)

Israel remembers its passage from misery to abundance, recalling that when it was enslaved in Egypt, the Lord saw its oppression and freed it, leading it to "a land flowing with milk and honey." In a memorial that weaves together history and nature, Israel acknowledges that the land on which it finds itself is a gift of God and for this reason it must proclaim a specific historical fact: "Today I declare to the LORD your God that I have come in to the land that the LORD swore to our ancestors to give us." The historical fact is recognized as the action of God: the Lord fulfilled the promise he had made. This acknowledgment is a true and proper confession of faith. "It is not a *claim*—'I own this land because I conquered it'—but an *acknowledgment*: 'I have come because God gave it.'"[3]

But the rite of the presentation of the firstfruits is not only a memorial of the past; it is also a memorial of the present, an appeal to Israel's responsibility in daily living. The passage of Deuteronomy ends with the ethical command of sharing: "Then you, together with the Levites and the aliens who reside among you, shall celebrate with all the bounty that the LORD your God has given to you and to your house" (Deut 26:11). What the Levite and the resident alien have in common is that they lack the right to possess land and therefore need to depend on the generosity of others. To command sharing with the Levites and resident aliens means to ask Israel to be for those who possess nothing, what God was for Israel when it was in Egypt without rights and in misery. The thanksgiving in presenting the fruits of the earth at the altar of the Lord "is not therefore the petty and egotistical joy of the one who 'enjoys' his piece of earth, but rather the gratitude of all and

---

3. Christopher J. H. Wright, *Deuteronomy* (Peabody, MA: Hendrickson, 1996), 271.

of each one for a gift to share . . . with the poor who lack the access to the fruits of the earth."[4]

In the Torah, Deuteronomy frequently offers bold legislation—the triennial tithe (Deut 14:1-18, 28-29; 26:12), the sabbatical year (Deut 15:7-11), the gleaning (Deut 24:19-21)—in order to guarantee that the poor have all that belongs to them by right, without having to beg for it. The hope for a just society derives from faith in God: "There will . . . be no one in need among you, because the LORD is sure to bless you in the land that the LORD your God is giving you as a possession to occupy" (Deut 15:4). From this grows a social structure, an economy of solidarity that serves as the foundation for a common justice, reflecting God's blessing on human work: "When you reap your harvest in your field and forget a sheaf in the field, you shall not go back to get it; it shall be left for the alien, the orphan, and the widow, so that the LORD your God may bless you in all your undertakings" (Deut 24:19). It is clear, then, that the offering of the firstfruits of the harvest is a ritual gesture that relativizes possession and puts some distance between the believer and the fruit of the land and of work, so that "in giving up part of what he has harvested, the believer confesses that he does not have absolute possession of his goods. Symbolically, the sacrificed offering, made holy by the sacrifice, was then shared."[5]

Worship of the Lord through the symbolic offering of the fruits of the earth is therefore authentic only when it is verified—in a sense, it is "made true"—by care for the

---

4. Antonio Bonora, "Dalla storia e dalla natura alla professione de fede e alla celebrazione (Deut 26:1-15)," *Parola, Spirito, e Vita* 25 (1992): 29.

5. D. Marguerat, "Pour une spiritualité de l'argent," *Lumière & Vie* 286 (2010): 37.

poor. This means that "it is in the ethical practice of sharing that the liturgy of Israel is thus accomplished. The rite
is the symbolic representation of the conjunction between
love of God and love of neighbor in which Israel will soon
discern . . . not only the central double commandment,
but also the very principle of the whole Law,"[6] the principle
that Jesus brings to the extreme in Mark's gospel: "Loving
God and loving one's neighbor is worth more than all the
holocausts and sacrifices" (cf. Mark 12:43).

Both in the Bible and in the history of religions, bringing
one's gifts to the altar is the act of worship *par excellence*,
and for this reason Jesus radicalizes the ethical responsibility inherent in worship to which the prophets of Israel
already had given voice:

> So when you are offering your gift at the altar, if you re-
> member that your brother or sister has something against
> you, leave your gift there before the altar and go; first be
> reconciled to your brother or sister, and then come and
> offer your gift. (Matt 5:23-24)

The exegete Jacques Dupont imagines the scene: "After
arriving at the temple with an offering . . . but before the
priest lays it upon the altar, the believer suddenly recalls
his brother, and his duty towards him interrupts the sacrificial process."[7] In the midst of presenting a gift at the
altar, the believer stops and leaves it there. The act of wor-

---

6. Louis-Marie Chauvet, *Symbol and Sacrament: A Sacramental
Reinterpretation of Christian Existence*, trans. Patrick Madigan and
Madeleine Beaumont (Collegeville, MN: Liturgical Press, 1995), 238.

7. Jacques Dupont, "'Laisse là ton offrande, devant l'autel . . .'
(Matt 5:23-24)," in *Traditio et Progressio. Studi liturgici in onore del
prof. Adrien Nocent*, ed. G. Farnedi (Rome: Pontifical Athenaeum of
Saint Anselm, 1988), 207–8.

ship is interrupted and reconciliation with the sister or brother comes first, for it is the condition of worship *sine qua non*. John Chrysostom notes the significance of the exact moment at which the sacrifice must be interrupted, putting into the mouth of God these words:

> "Let my service," God says, "be interrupted, that your love may continue, since your being reconciled to thy brother is also a sacrifice." For this reason, God did not say "after the offering" or "before the offering." Rather, while the very gift lies there, and when the sacrifice is already beginning, God sends you to be reconciled to your brother, not after removing the sacrifice which lies before us, nor before presenting the gift, but while it lies before us, he sends you out.[8]

The image of an offering abandoned before the altar while the offerer goes to reconcile with someone is a bit upsetting perhaps. But Jesus' thinking is clear: if the worship we offer is the moment in which we make memorial of the primacy of God in our lives, then it is authentic only if it is also a memorial of our sisters and brothers and what we hold against them. Otherwise, this making memorial of God is accompanied by forgetting our sisters and brothers and the evil they have done, and it would become complicit in the injustice. Ritual worship is not abolished but suspended, so that it might represent the truth of what is celebrated and of superabundant justice. The *Mishna* attributes to Rabbi Eleazar ben Azaria this teaching:

> For transgressions that are between man and God the Day of Atonement effects atonement, but for transgressions

---

8. John Chrysostom, *Homilies on the Gospel of Saint Matthew* (Oxford: James Parker and Co, 1876), 16.12, p. 206.

that are between a man and his fellow the Day of Atonement effects atonement only if he has appeased his fellow.[9]

Jesus' radicalization of the ethical command suggested by the presentation of the offering at the altar can be expressed in these terms: it is better not to participate in the ritual act, in the Eucharist, than to participate in a way that negates in practice what is celebrated in the rite.

Augustine, too, commenting on the passage of Matthew, insists on the necessity of interrupting and postponing one's worship, affirming the primacy of charity:

> God won't be angry because you delay in placing your gift on the altar; God wants you much more than your gift. I mean, if still bearing a bitter grudge against your brother, you arrive with a gift at your God's place, he will answer you, "You're lost, what have you brought me? You are offering your gift, and you are not a gift to God yourself [*offers munus tuum et tu non es munus Dei*]." Christ wants one he has redeemed with his blood much more than he wants what you have found in your storehouse.[10]

With these words, Augustine recalls the most genuinely Christian truth about the Eucharist, which is that when we make an offering, we offer ourselves. By presenting our gifts at the altar, we place ourselves on the altar. "[W]e ourselves," Augustine writes, "are his best and most noble sacrifice, and it is the mystery of this sacrifice that we celebrate in our offerings."[11] If our own mystery is placed on the altar, what we are in truth before God is revealed in

9. Yoma 8.9, in *The Mishnah*, trans. Herbert Danby (Oxford: Oxford University Press, 1933), 172.

10. St. Augustine, Sermon 82.5, in *Sermons*, part 3, vol. 3, trans. Edmund Hill (Brooklyn: New City Press, 1991), 371–72.

11. St. Augustine, *The City of God*, 19.23, trans. William Babcock (Hyde Park, NY: New City Press, 2013), 384.

the quality of our relationship with our neighbor. That means that one cannot be at the same time one who offers and one who gives offense—making an offering to God and giving offense to one's neighbor. We simply cannot present our entire life as a gift to God at the altar if we live this life without our neighbor or against our neighbor.

There is no altar of the Lord that is not at the same time a memorial of the altar that is our neighbor. For this reason the *Didascalia* commands Christians: "[T]he widows and orphans are to be considered among you as a type of the altar."[12] This Christian understanding of the essential relationship between the altar and the poor finds its highest epiphany in the liturgy. We should note, in fact, that until about the ninth century, the faithful brought gifts to church to be distributed to the poor, and from these gifts were taken the bread and wine that were put on the altar for the Eucharist; the offering to God and the offering to the poor form a single act of offering, attributing the same sacrificial value to both offerings. How could we not recall here that the apostle Paul understands the collection for the poor of Jerusalem as a liturgy and that in the Second Letter to the Corinthians he writes: "The rendering of this ministry [*diakonía tês leitourgías*] not only supplies the needs of the saints but also overflows with many thanksgivings to God" (2 Cor 9:12). We find this same vision of the collection attested to in the earliest account of a Christian Eucharist (around the year 150), provided by Justin in his first apology:

12. Alistair Stewart-Sykes, *The Didascalia Apostolorum: An English Version*, chap. 9 (Turnhout, Belgium: Brepols, 2009), 151. See also Polycarp of Smyrna: "Teach the widows . . . that they are an altar of God," Letter to the Philippians 4 in *The Apostolic Fathers*, trans. Francis X. Glimm, et al. (Washington, DC: Catholic University of America Press, 1962), 137.

And those who prosper, and so wish, contribute what each thinks fit; and what is collected is deposited with the Ruler, who takes care of the orphans and widows, and those who, on account of sickness or any other cause, are in want, and those who are in bonds, and the strangers who are sojourners among us, and in a word [He] is the guardian of all those in need.[13]

Although Justin makes no mention of a rite of presentation of gifts, it is essential to note that the collection for the poor is a liturgical act and that the one who presides over the community's eucharistic offering also presides over the charitable offering for the poor.

## The Presentation of Gifts, Image and Paradigm of a Eucharistic Ethic

In the light of these reflections, we can now consider a little more closely the rite of the presentation of the gifts of the *Ordo missae* of the Missal of Paul VI. In the GIRM, we read:

At the Preparation of the Gifts, bread and wine with water are brought to the altar, the same elements, that is to say, which Christ took into his hands.[14]

At the beginning of the Liturgy of the Eucharist the gifts which will become Christ's Body and Blood are brought to the altar. . . . It is a praiseworthy practice for the bread and wine to be presented by the faithful. They are

13. Justin Martyr, "The First Apology," 67, in *The First and Second Apologies*, trans. Leslie William Barnard, Ancient Christian Writers, 56 (Mahwah, NJ: Paulist Press, 1997), 71.

14. *General Instruction for the Roman Missal*, n. 72.

then accepted at an appropriate place by the Priest or the Deacon to be carried to the altar.[15]

It is desirable that the participation of the faithful be expressed by an offering, whether of bread and wine for the celebration of the Eucharist or of other gifts to relieve the needs of the Church and of the poor.[16]

Let us consider three questions in light of the vision presented in the GIRM: "*Quis praesentat?*" (Who presents the gifts?), "*Quid praesentatur?*" (What is presented?), and "*Cui praesentatur?*" (To whom are they presented?). The three answers will tell us about the subject, the object, and the receiver of the rite of preparation of the gifts.

## "*Quis presentat?*"

The GIRM is clear: "It is a praiseworthy practice for the bread and wine to be presented by the faithful." The subject of the presentation of the gifts, then, is the faithful who gather in assembly, and although this rite is carried out materially by just two or three of them, this is symbolic, because in reality each member of the assembly is called to bring gifts to the altar, in obedience to the command of Moses: "They shall not appear before the LORD empty-handed" (Deut 16:16). No believer may come before the altar with empty hands, because the vocation of every person is to offer the world to God by her own hands. The subject of the presentation of the gifts is every one of the faithful, because in this gesture is accomplished the priestly act to which each person is called. Orthodox theology in particular has meditated on this truth. The Greek theologian and bishop John Zizioulas has written:

15. Ibid., n. 73.
16. Ibid., n. 140.

"[In the hands of the human person] the world is raised up to infinite possibility, being referred to God and offered to him as 'God's property.' This constitutes the base of what we call the *priesthood of the human person*; taking the world in his hands, integrating it creatively and referring it to God, the person frees creation from its limits and brings it to its fullness."[17] Another Orthodox theologian, Alexander Schmemann, wrote,

> "*Homo sapiens*," "*homo faber*" . . . yes, but, first of all, "*homo adorans*." The first, the basic definition of man is that he is *the priest*. He stands in the center of the world and unifies it in his act of blessing God, of both receiving the world from God and offering it to God—and by filling the world with this Eucharist, he transforms his life, the one that he receives from the world, into life in God, into communion with Him. The world was created as the "matter," the material of one all-embracing Eucharist, and man was created as the priest of this cosmic sacrament.[18]

The priesthood of man is therefore primarily an existential stance that finds in the liturgy its full sacramental epiphany. Every member of the assembly who takes part symbolically in the presentation of the gifts brings to fulfillment the journey through which she lays her entire life on the altar, bringing before the Lord the fruit of her encounter with creation, because she too is part of God's creation. She too is the fruit of nature, of history, of culture, and of that uninterrupted work of humanization which others have carried out before her and which she continues. In

---

17. John Zizioulas, *Il creato come eucaristia* (Bose: Qiqajon, 1994), 67.

18. Alexander Schmemann, *For the Life of the World*, 2nd ed. (Crestwood, NY: St. Vladimir's Seminary Press, 1973), 15.

the bread and the wine that is brought to the altar so that it might become, through the epiclesis of the Spirit, the body and blood of the Lord, the entire life of humanity is also transformed, through the work of sanctification, into an offering to God and neighbor, into an act of communion and an act of sharing.

### *"Quid praesentatur?"*

The GIRM notes the object of the presentation of gifts and the reason for offering these gifts rather than others: "At the Preparation of the Gifts, bread and wine with water are brought to the altar, the same elements, that is to say, which Christ took into his hands."[19] Because Christ took bread and wine in his hands, bread and wine are brought to the altar. It is a simple criteria that, when observed, spares the assembly all kinds of improvised choices and meanings that usually tend to be more allegorical representations than authentic liturgical symbols.

Why did Jesus choose the bread and wine as the two realities that convey, better than anything else, the meaning of the gift of his life unto death, the two realities that would become, from that moment, his body and his blood? It will be helpful, in answering this question, to consider the *berakhot*, the blessings spoken over the bread and wine. These two formulas of Jewish inspiration certainly represent one of the most innovative and expressive novelties of the *ordo missae* of the Missal of Paul VI:

> Blessed are you, Lord God of all creation,
> for through your goodness we have received
> the bread we offer you:
> fruit of the earth and work of human hands,
> it will become for us the bread of life.

---

19. GIRM, n. 72.

> Blessed are you, Lord God of all creation,
> for through your goodness we have received
> the wine we offer you:
> fruit of the vine and work of human hands,
> it will become our spiritual drink.[20]

"Blessed are you, Lord": in the liturgy, the bread and the wine are not blessed; rather, the Lord is blessed by these gifts. It is quite significant that the Lord is blessed using the appellative, *Deus universi*, God of the universe, "God of all creation." Though it is true that all food is in some way symbolic of the whole, this can be said of bread in a unique way, so that Pythagoras could say, "The universe begins with bread."[21] In bread, we can recognize the fundamental elements of the world: the earth that receives seed and makes it grow, the water and finely ground grain mixed together into a dough, and the fire and air for baking. Honorius of Autun expresses well the idea that bread is a symbol of all that nourishes us and helps us live when he suggests—though inaccurately from an etymological standpoint—that the term for *bread* in the romance languages (*panem, pane, pan, pain*) is derived from the Greek *pân*, meaning "all." "*Pân* means *all*," he writes, "and therefore bread is offered because total salvation is received."[22]

Invoking the God of the universe, we recognize in bread the *beginning*, that is, the most basic human sustenance. Bread is always, in all languages and cultures, a metaphor for food. To lack bread means to lack food, to lack that on which we depend to live and without which we die for lack of nourishment.

---

20. *The Roman Missal*, 529.
21. Cited in P. Matvejevic, *Pane Nostro* (Milan: Garzanti, 2010), 17.
22. Onorio di Autun, *La Gemma dell'Anima* I, 99, PL 172, 576.

Wine, unlike bread, is not a principle of sustenance. It is not on the order of necessity. Without wine, one can certainly live. Enzo Bianchi has written:

> Along with the bread we need, the daily bread that dispels hunger and that is necessary for survival, we have wine of gratuity and feast: a drink that is never necessary simply to live, but which still is precious for the consolation, the shared joy, and the friendship that it helps to foster.[23]

> Wine, then, is gratuity, joy, pleasure, and at times also excess, the kind of excess which removes some of the burden of the drudgery of daily living and calms the heart. . . . Certainly wine calls for caution and responsibility, and there is an art to drinking it to the point of gentle intoxication that frees one from the composure that daily living demands without succumbing to unrestrained drunkenness.[24]

Wine is therefore a symbol of gratuity, expressing the excess of human life. It is synonymous with feasting and fullness of life. Because its context is joy, wine calls to mind community, sharing, and social bonds. Both bread and wine are synonymous with sharing, because the human person does not eat and drink simply as the animals do but shares with others that which brings life and joy. Thus Predrag Matvejevic describes the feast that bread creates, the celebration of life it fosters: "Taken from the oven and brought to the table, bread announces a feast for the family who gathers around it, for the mother who has baked

---

23. Enzo Bianchi, *Il Pane di Ieri* (Turin: Einaudi, 2008), 50.
24. Enzo Bianchi, *Ognio Cosa all Sua Stagione* (Turin: Einaudi, 2010), 37–38.

it, for the father who has earned it, for the children it will feed."[25]

Bread and wine are brought to the altar together, never one without the other, because together they are the sign that human life, when it is fully humanized, includes both the daily and the festive, necessity and gratuity, fatigue and joy, need and excess, moderation and inebriation, temperance and euphoria, obedience and freedom. For this reason, the blessing recognizes that "through your goodness we have received the bread . . . the wine," confessing that it is *de tua largitate,* from the generosity of God that we receive bread and wine; they are gifts. The great litany of psalm 136 concludes by acknowledging: "[The LORD] gives bread to all flesh / for his mercy endures forever" (Ps 136:25 NABRE).

Augustine's address to the neophytes places the journey of their initiation in the context of the history of bread, to the point of being able to say that the Christian is made like bread is made:

> Call to mind what this created object was, not so long ago, in the fields; how the earth produced it, the rain nourished it, ripened it into the full ear; then human labor carried it to the threshing floor, threshed it, winnowed it, stored it, brought it out, ground it, mixed it into dough, baked it, and hardly any time ago at all produced it finally as bread. Now call yourselves also to mind: you didn't exist, and you were created, you were carried to the Lord's threshing floor, you were threshed by the labor of oxen, that is of the preachers of the gospel. When, as catechumens, you were being held back, you were being stored in the barn. You gave in your names; then you began to be ground by fasts and exorcisms. Afterward you came to the water, and you were moistened into dough,

25. Matvejevic, *Pane Nostro*, 190.

and made into one lump. With the application of the heat
of the Holy Spirit you were baked, and made into the
Lord's loaf of bread.[26]

But the bread, gift of God, is "fruit of the earth and work of
human hands" and the wine "fruit of the vine and work of
human hands." It is a very concrete image—*operis manum
hominem*—seeing our hands as the first and indispensable
tool of our work. In the case of bread, the hands play a
fundamental role in its preparation. Hands not only mix the
flower and water; they also shape the form of bread. Many
people still today, before baking their bread, trace a cross
on the dough, which is at the same time a Christian sign
and an imprint of the hands that made the bread, while "in
some Islamic countries the one who bakes it pokes her
thumb into the dough before baking it, as if to confirm it
was made by human hands."[27]

Bread and wine are fruits of the earth. Psalm 104 proclaims to the Lord:

> You . . . bring forth food from the earth,
> and wine to gladden the human heart . . .
> and bread to strengthen the human heart. (Ps 104:14-15)

And yet bread and wine are not found in nature. The
grain and the grapes must be taken from the earth. They
are not only, as the liturgical blessing says, "fruit of the
earth" but also "work of human hands." The relationship
between bread and work recalls first of all that bread is
the result of man's efforts to cultivate the earth, efforts that
come as a result of the curse on the soil caused by Adam's

---

26. St. Augustine, Sermon 229.1, in *Sermons*, part 3, vol. 6, trans.
Edmund Hill (New Rochelle, NY: New City Press, 1993), 265. This
image is repeated in Sermon 229A.2, in ibid., 270.

27. Matvejevic, *Pane Nostro*, 22.

disobedience: "By the sweat of your face you shall eat bread" (Gen 3:19). The Psalmist speaks of "eating the bread of anxious toil" (Ps 127:2).

Fruits "of the earth and work of human hands," bread and wine are products not only of nature but of human culture. The Hebrew verb *'avad* means "to work," "to cultivate," and also "to serve" in the double meaning of the hard work of a slave and the service of God in liturgy. The Hebrew *'avad* corresponds to the Latin verb *colere*, which expresses the same thing: in its primary meaning, cultivating and the work of cultivation, and in its secondary meaning, cult, the act of worship.[28] From *colere* also derives *culture*, which is both the work of civilization and the work of humanization. Both the Hebrew and the Latin words therefore express the relationship that unites cultivation of the earth, worship, and culture, demonstrating that in the act of obedience to the command received by God to cultivate the earth, humanity makes of work an act that is both cultic and cultural. That is, it is both a glorification of God and a humanization of humanity. The human person thus collaborates, as Olivier Clement writes, in the salvation of the world:

> In the work that encompasses scientific knowledge and technical know-how, man is called to collaborate with God for the salvation of the universe. It is above all here that the Christian must be a liturgical person. There are no frontiers in the radiation of the liturgy. We are priests and kings, and in the awareness of nature as in its transformation, we live the great cosmic Eucharist: "From the gifts we have received from you, we offer completely and for all."[29]

28. Cf. Claus Westermann, "Lavoro e attività culturale nella Bibbia," *Concilium* 1 (1980): 120.

29. Olivier Clement, *Il Senso della Terra* (Rome: Lipa, 2007), 68.

In the history of humanity, in fact, there has never been nature without culture. For as long as humanity has existed, it has never existed in pure animality, including in its relationship with the earth. For people, the earth was never virgin land: there was always culture, even in its more crude and primitive forms. To make bread, people must till the land, plant seeds, harvest the grain, beat it, grind it into flour, knead it with water, and then bake it. In the same way, to make wine, people must plant a vine, attend to it year after year, harvest the grapes, press them, and then all sorts of special skills and knowledge are necessary! Bread and wine are "fruit of the earth and work of human hands" because they are not static material but fruit of the dynamism and creativity of people that is always both necessity and effort, civility and culture, duty and celebration. For the believer, work reaches its fullness in the act of worship, the bringing of the bread and wine to the altar and pronouncing over them the blessing that is a celebration of the covenant stipulated between God, humanity, and nature.[30]

## "Cui praesentatur?"

Over the bread, the blessing says we offer it to God, that "it will become for us the bread of life." We offer the wine, too, to God, that "it will become our spiritual drink." The text is clear: the bread and wine are presented to the Lord, placed in his presence, or, in biblical language, brought before his face.[31] And yet, the blessing itself says that the Lord is not the ultimate recipient of the gifts, for it says we present them so that they become *for us* bread of life and

---

30. Cf. Edward Foley, Kathleen Hughes and Gilbert Ostdiek, "The Preparatory Rites: A Case Study in Liturgical Ecology," *Worship* 67, no. 1 (1993): 17–38.

31. The German Missal says they are brought *"Vor dein Angesicht."*

spiritual drink. If we take seriously that "for us" (*ex quo nobis* in the Latin text, which means literally "from which will be to us"), we understand that the ultimate recipients of the gifts are the same faithful who brought the gifts to the altar. The thinking here becomes more complex, but it is essential to understand this dynamic in order to understand the radical newness of Christian worship with respect to the sacrificial Jewish economy and that of the pagans.

It is often pointed out, and rightly so, that the conciliar liturgical reform called this first moment of the Liturgy of the Eucharist "the presentation of gifts," rather than "offertory," because the sacramental offering takes place in the eucharistic prayer. But calling this rite the "presentation of the gifts" means affirming that the bread and wine are presented to the Lord so that God may send the Spirit upon them to sanctify them and make them the body and blood of Jesus Christ. This, too, is affirmed in the blessing: "the bread we offer you . . . it will become for us the bread of life. . . . the wine we offer you . . . will become our spiritual drink" (*panis vitae, potus spiritualis*). In sum, the bread and wine are not brought to the altar so that the Lord may be nourished. Irenaeus of Lyons writes: "We offer to God not as to one who has need of our offerings, but to give him thanks for his gifts and to sanctify creation."[32] The gifts are placed on the altar that God may sanctify them by the power of the Spirit and make them "for us" bread of life and spiritual drink. And so the bread that the faithful have carried in their hands to the altar, after thanks has been given, are then taken from the altar and placed anew in the hands of the faithful as the body of Christ.

But we still have not fully answered the question, "To whom are the gifts presented?" The GIRM notes: "It is

---

32. Irenaeus, *Against Heresies*, 4.18.6. [My translation from the Italian.—Trans.]

desirable that the participation of the faithful be expressed by an offering, whether of bread and wine for the celebration of the Eucharist or of other gifts to relieve the needs of the Church and of the poor."

The participation of the faithful in the presentation of the gifts is not, then, limited to bringing bread and wine for the Eucharist; it includes bringing "other gifts to relieve the needs of the Church and of the poor." And so the entire Christian community, and particularly the poor, are the recipients of the presentation of the fruits of the earth and of the human work that forms them, which both remain incomplete until, through the epiclesis, they reach their *pléroma*, their fullness of meaning. Jean Corbon, with his characteristic spiritual profundity, writes:

> What we offer at the threshold of the anaphora is not gifts but an incompleteness, an appeal (the epiclesis is a groaning), the anxious expectation of creation that carries the imprint of our hands but not yet the imprint of the light.
>
> For this light that transfigures both work and the created thing which work shapes is the light of communion. Like the eucharistic liturgy, the Eucharist as lived out in daily life is crowned by communion. . . . It incites to sharing, for since all the earth belongs to God, the fruit of human labor is meant for all the children of God. Sharing is the "jubilee year" of work, and Sunday, the day of abstention from activity, is the day on which all work is restored to its purity through gratuitousness; laborious work is for the sake of bread, and Sunday bread, "the bread of this Day," is for the sake of the transfiguration of work.[33]

The presentation of the gifts, then, is an image and paradigm of a eucharistic ethic. Just as the ritual gesture

---

33. Jean Corbon, *The Wellspring of Worship* (New York: Paulist Press, 1988), 160–61.

of presenting the firstfruits of the earth was, for every
Israelite, both a memorial of the past and a call to responsibility in the present, so in the same way the rite of
the presentation of the gifts is for every Christian a memorial of the offering of Christ on the cross and a call to
ethical responsibility in the *hodie* of the church, society,
and the entire world.

## The Eucharist, Source of Social Transformation

In concluding this reflection, we must ask ourselves: Are
Christians today aware of the relationship that exists between our eucharistic praxis and the praxis of charity offered to people in need? Do they understand the Eucharist
as a source of social transformation?

Every Sunday, Christians are called to carry out the rite
of the presentation of the gifts with ever-greater awareness
that the Eucharist is the foundation of a still unfulfilled
hope: the communion of all humanity in its social, ethnic,
and cultural diversity. It is impossible for believers truly to
celebrate the Eucharist without an awareness of being part
of a system that is not only economic and political but also
cultural and religious, a system of values and behaviors, of
choices and judgments that has for centuries now created
poverty and oppression in the world and robbed people not
only of bread but of justice and dignity. Challenged by the
situations of millions of men and women, Christians who
live in the West are called to reconsider the way in which,
from the end of the Second World War up to our own day,
they have celebrated and adored the Eucharist, which is
*nutrimentum caritatis*, "the food of charity."[34]

34. Prayer after Communion, Twenty-Second Sunday in Ordinary
Time, *The Roman Missal*, 482.

It is not possible to close our eyes to the most recent data on food waste: in the Western world, from 1974 to today, food waste increased by 50 percent. In a civil nation like Switzerland, an ordinary family throws away about 25 percent of the food it buys.[35] This attests to a truth: what is not shared is wasted, confirming the words of psalm 49:

> Mortals cannot abide in their pomp;
> they are like animals that perish. (Ps 49:13)

Are Christians aware of the gap that still very much exists between sacramental practice and the practice of justice?

The liturgy offers a challenge to the church in the world that makes Christians, perhaps more today than ever before, debtors before all humanity. In a society dominated by the strongest among us, the Eucharist is a real threat. In a society where individualism triumphs, the Eucharist reminds us of the common destiny of all humanity. In a society where waste prevails, the Eucharist is a call to share. The Eucharist forges a theology of charity, for charity is a mystery that is both sacramental and prophetic. The Eucharist is a reality that is as social as it is theological. It is the crucible of an ethic of service of humanity.

---

35. Cf. Antonio Cianciullo, "Troppo cibo nella spazzatura. Le mosse anti-spreco delle città," *La Repubblica* (July 12, 2010): 20.

# Part Two

# Liturgy in the Life of the Church

# Chapter Five

# The Sacrament of the Assembly

*"I will not believe that [you are a Christian], nor count you among Christians, until I see you in Christ's church."*

—Augustine of Hippo[1]

## *The Liturgical Assembly Poses Questions to the Church*

The liturgical assembly is the fundamental and original form of the church, for it is through the assembly that the church expresses to itself and to the world its nature, its purpose, its mission, and its role in history.[2] The eucharistic ecclesiology expressed by the council in *Sacrosanctum Concilium* recognized that "the principal manifestation

1. St. Augustine, *The Confessions* 8.4, trans. Maria Boulding (Hyde Park, NY: New City Press, 1997), 187.
2. This chapter was originally published as *Il sacramento dell'assemblea. L'assemblea liturgica il nostro modo de essere chiesa,* Testi di meditazione 118 (Bose: Qiqajon, 2004).

of the church consists in the full, active participation of all God's holy people in the same liturgical celebrations."[3] For this reason, to explore the theme of the assembly means to consider the essence of the Christian experience of believing, the foundation of Christianity, and the conditions of its continued existence in history.

We see in the West today real difficulties in the ordinary experience of the church. We see signs of weariness, fatigue, and discomfort on the faces of those who make up the Christian community. Christianity seems to have lost its momentum, to the point that many now wonder about its future, about the survival of Christianity in the West. We need only note the titles of some recent French publications: Maurice Bellet's *La quatrième hypothèse: Sur l'avenir du christianisme*[4] [The Fourth Hypothesis: On the Future of Christianity]; Marc Lienhard's "Le christianisme a-t-il un avenir?"[5] [Does Christianity Have a Future?]; Christian Duquoc's *Christianisme: Memoire pour l'avenire*[6] [Christianity: Memory of the Future]; and Albert Rouet's, *La chance d'un christianisme fragile*[7] [The Chance of a Fragile Christianity]. Each of these authors asks, in one way or another, the same question: "Are we perhaps the last Christians?" In seeking to discern whether Christianity can survive in the West, each of them emphasizes that one of the conditions essential for the future of Christianity is the full

---

3. Second Vatican Council, *Sacrosanctum Concilium*, n. 41.

4. M. Bellet, *La quatrième hypothèse: Sur l'avenir du christianisme* (Paris: DDB, 2001).

5. M. Lienhard, "Le christianisme a-t-il un avenir?," in *Histoire et herméneuticque. Mélanges pour Gottfried Hammann*, ed. M. Rose (Geneva: Labor et fides, 2002), 237–47.

6. C. Duquoc, *Christianisme. Mémoire pour l'avenir* (Paris: Cerf, 2000).

7. A. Rouet, *La chance d'un christianisme fragile. Entretiens avec Yves de Gentil-Baichis* (Paris: Bayard, 2001).

understanding of the value and the meaning of the Sunday eucharistic gathering. The conviction that emerges from these texts is that this gathering is an essential experience that must never be abandoned, because it is a constitutive element of Christianity and its identity.

To reflect on the theme of assembly from the liturgical point of view means above all to affirm that the *lex orandi* cannot be limited simply to being the law of faith; it must also constitute the church's law of being and acting. In other words, how the church prays establishes not only what the church believes but what the church *is*. The nature of our liturgies depend very much on the model of church that they express, since, as John Paul II wrote in *Dominicae Cenae*, "A very close and organic bond exists between the renewal of the liturgy and the renewal of the whole life of the Church. The Church not only acts but also expresses herself in the liturgy, lives by the liturgy and draws from the liturgy the strength for her life."[8] If how the church prays determines what the church is, we should ask ourselves what our liturgical assemblies say about our way of being church. We must understand that the structure and the dynamic of the liturgical assembly become the structure and dynamic of the life of the church. Our reflections here will focus, therefore, on the structure and the dynamic of the liturgical assembly, which includes three successive moments:

1. God calls his people together
2. God speaks to his people
3. God enters into a covenant with his people

8. Pope John Paul II, *Dominicae Cenae*, n. 13. Available at http://www.vatican.va/holy_father/john_paul_ii/letters/documents/hf_jp-ii_let_24021980_dominicae-cenae_en.html, accessed November 17, 2013.

## God Calls His People Together

In order to understand the nature of liturgy well, it is important that we consider first of all the act that is the foundation of every other liturgical action. Christian liturgy happens when the people of God gather. The condition for the possibility of every liturgy is the gathering of the people. To say there can be no liturgy without gathering is not to suggest the primacy of the assembly in itself, in some populist sense. Rather, it is to insist on the primacy of the action of God. God calls his people, and those who respond to this call gather together in his presence. The liturgical assembly is not, most fundamentally, the "self-gathering" of believers. The origin of every liturgy is the call of God and the response of the people. For this reason, the first and fundamental liturgical action (in the etymological sense of *leitourgía*, "action of the people") is the people's response to God's call by gathering as an assembly. We must repeat with emphasis: the celebration of the Christian faith is first of all *opus Dei*—to borrow the expression used by Benedict in his Rule to refer to common prayer—inasmuch as it is founded uniquely upon the action and the call of God. The people respond to this call by gathering again in assembly: this is the first liturgical action of the people. If there is no response to the call, there is no assembly and therefore no liturgy. By definition, the gathering together of Christians in assembly is the primordial *actio liturgica*.

To understand the gathering as primordial *actio liturgica* is to go to the biblical roots of the assembly of the people of God and to draw from there its meaning. In a particular way, it brings us to the assembly of Sinai (see Exod 24:1-11), the image of every assembly of Israel and therefore of every Christian assembly. It is that assembly that Luke, in the Acts of the Apostles, calls "the church in the desert" (*he ekklesía en tê eremo*: Acts 7:38),[9] an expression that Jerome translated as "the church in solitude." The description of the Sinai assembly in Exodus 24 testifies that the calling together of Israel is God's initiative, for it is by God's free decision that this people will be God's "treasured possession out of all the peoples . . . a priestly kingdom and a holy nation" (Exod 19:5-6). It is in the name of God and by God's mandate that Moses calls the people together (Exod 19:7) to prepare a liturgical assembly that will be an *encounter* with God (Exod 19:10-11).

The Hebrew text of Scripture speaks of the assembly as *qahal*. This noun derives from the root *q h l* ("to call"). The Septuagint translation of the Bible into Greek regularly renders the term *qahal* as *ekklesía*, in the cultic sense; for the Septuagint, the *ekklesía* is the liturgical assembly of the children of Israel called by God. *Ekklesía* is a noun composed of the preposition *ek*, "from," and the verb *kaléo*, "to call." *Ekklesía* is, therefore, the "convocation," the "calling forth from" and, in the middle form of the verb *kaléo*, "those called together."

The first three times the word *ekklesía* appears in the Greek Bible, it is in the context of a phrase that is typical of Deuteronomy: "the day of the assembly" or "the day of the church" (*he heméra tês ekklesías*: Deut 4:10; 9:10; 18:16), which is absent in the Masoretic text. The church-assembly of Deuteronomy is the convocation of Sinai at which Moses speaks, according to the text of the Septuagint, these words:

> When I went up the mountain to receive the stone tablets,
> the tablets of the covenant that the LORD made with you,

9. It is helpful to recall that the Jewish title of the book of Numbers is *In the Desert*. In his homilies on this book, Origen offers a Christian interpretation of the "church of the desert," constructing a true ecclesiology of the desert.

> I remained on the mountain forty days and forty nights;
> I neither ate bread nor drank water. And the LORD gave
> me the two stone tablets written with the finger of God;
> on them were all the words that the LORD had spoken to
> you at the mountain out of the fire on the day of the as-
> sembly. (Deut 9:9-10)

Choosing to render the word *qahal* in the Masoretic text
with the expression *he heméra tês ekklesías*, the Septuagint
clearly intends to say that the assembly called together to
hear the word of the Lord amidst the flames of fire is not
a generic meeting but the highest manifestation of the mystery of the people that God calls together; that convocation
becomes a liturgical assembly. Here we find an expression
of the idea that it is the Word of God that calls, that gathers
the community and constitutes Israel as "church." "The
day of the church" is, therefore, the day on which God calls
the children of Israel into holy assembly and gives them
the tablets of the Law in order to establish the covenant.

The Christian liturgy has faithfully preserved this biblical conception of the assembly, affirming that the church
is the place where the people of God is gathered. Suffice
it here to point out one particular element of liturgical
practice that reveals this truth. The norms that regulate
the liturgy indicate that the bishop or the presbyter who
presides at a liturgy does not enter the sanctuary to greet
or receive the Christians as they gather to worship but that
he approaches it only after the assembly has gathered. In
the GIRM we read, "When the people are gathered [*populo
congregato*], and as the Priest enters with the Deacon and
ministers, the Entrance Chant begins."[10] John Chrysostom
attests to the antiquity of this liturgical sign, commenting,
"[T]he church is the common home of all, and after all of

---

10. GIRM, n. 47.

you have first occupied it, we enter in. . . . we also pronounce 'peace' in common to all, directly as we enter."[11]

For Chrysostom, the *ekklesía* is not the bishop's house but the house of the people of God, and so he is not to greet those who gather there like the head of a house might greet guests. Christians who gather in assembly are not the guests of the one who presides, Chrysostom insists. Rather, they are gathered in their own house: "The church is the common home of all." In other words, the ordained minister presides over the assembly but does not precede the assembly, inasmuch as he is also a member of the assembly. He too comes in response to the call of God to gather. He too confesses his sins, hears the Word of God proclaimed, offers thanksgiving, and is nourished by the body and blood of the Lord in order to become, with the members of the community he serves, one body in Christ.

At the foundation of this rubric is an important biblical truth and a particular understanding of the church. *Populo congregato*: the gathering of the people is the first *actio liturgica*. The liturgy does not begin with the opening song or the sign of the cross but with God calling together the people and the people responding to this call by gathering in assembly. The entrance of the ordained minister into the midst of the *populo congregato* is the liturgical sign that attests that the assembly gathered is not merely *opus hominis* but first of all *opus Dei*. It is not the bishop or the presbyter who calls Christians together, and not the people who initiate the gathering themselves; it is God who calls together, with his Word, men and women in holy community.

11. John Chrysostom, *Homilies on the Gospel of Saint Matthew* 32, 9, Nicene and Post-Nicene Fathers 10, ed. Philip Schaff (Grand Rapids, MI: Eerdmans, repr. 1991), 216.

The truth of this sign must permeate the entire liturgical action and not only the entrance of the ordained minister. It is worth noting that the orientation in the current liturgy, with the presbyter continually standing or sitting face to face with the assembly, can threaten to obfuscate the theological truth of the Christian assembly. It is God who calls together those who gather, and they gather, before all else, in the presence of God. Often today, the position and the dimensions of the presbyter's chair represent a serious theological problem. While it is true that in the Roman basilicas, as well as in the ancient Syriac churches, the episcopal throne is located in the center of the apse and facing the people, it is also true that the parish churches never had a central chair. Suffice it to recall that in the sanctuary of Tridentine churches, both the episcopal throne and the presbyter's chair were originally to the side, not at the center. In Eastern churches, too, the bishop's throne is not central; it is located outside the sanctuary, beside the iconostasis.

The gathering of the people of God in assembly is the first and primordial eucharistic act; it is already an act of thanksgiving. We can therefore make our own the expression coined by the Russian Orthodox theologian Alexander Schmemann, in which he defines the Eucharist as "the sacrament of the assembly."[12]

### God Speaks to His People

In the fourth chapter of Deuteronomy, Moses says to the people of Israel gathered in assembly at Sinai, "[Remember] how you once stood before the LORD your God at

---

12. Alexander Schmemann, *The Eucharist: Sacrament of the Kingdom*, trans. Paul Kachur (Crestwood, NY: St. Vladimir's Seminary Press, 1987), 11–26.

Horeb, when the LORD said to me, 'Assemble the people for me, and I will let them hear my words'" (Deut 4:10). God calls his people through his Word and the people become an *ekklesía*, an assembly. The Word of God is a gathering word. It is truly the *davar* that does not return to the Lord empty, without accomplishing that for which it was sent (cf. Isa 55:11). The first result of God speaking is a people gathered to hear his Word; the Word begins as the subject of the convocation and then becomes the object of the convocation. In the liturgy of the covenant, Moses writes the words of the Lord in the book of the covenant: "Then he took the book of the covenant, and read it in the hearing of the people; and they said, 'All that the LORD has spoken we will do, and we will be obedient'" (Exod 24:7). Hearing the word of God is what makes Israel the people of God, which is why God says through the prophet Jeremiah, "[T]his command I gave them, 'Obey my voice, and I will be your God, and you shall be my people'" (Jer 7:23).

Like Israel, the Christian community too is constituted by the Word of God: "They preached the word of truth, and through it they begot churches,"[13] Augustine says in reference to the preaching of the apostles. The proclamation of the word of God gives birth to the church, and for this reason the liturgical assembly is the vital and true home of the Scriptures.

The liturgical reform of Vatican II insisted that no sacrament can be celebrated without a Liturgy of the Word, because a sacrament is the crystallization, the visibility, of the Word.[14] In the episode of Jesus preaching in the

---

13. St. Augustine, *Expositions of the Psalms 33–50*, trans. Maria Boulding (Hyde Park, NY: New City Press, 2000), 301.

14. To use Augustine's classic expression: "*Accedit verbum ad elementum, et fit sacramentum, etiam ipsum tamquam visibile*

synagogue of Nazareth, narrated in the Gospel of Luke (cf.
Luke 4:16-22), we find the image of every Liturgy of the
Word, because it expresses the four constitutive elements
of the Judeo-Christian Liturgy of the Word:

a) the received, canonical texts of the Bible are read
   aloud;
b) these texts are proclaimed as the living word of God
   for today;
c) they are proclaimed to an assembly that recognizes in
   them its own identity;
d) the assembly is led by an authority who testifies to the
   foundational authenticity (in the case of the Christian
   liturgy, the apostolic authenticity) of what has been
   read.[15]

This is the dynamic by which the word of God is proclaimed to the community through the use of a book. The
*ekklesía* is therefore the vital and true home of Scripture,
insofar as the liturgical assembly is the place where the
biblical texts are proclaimed, that is, *read for* an assembly
gathered by a word—the Word of God, who calls the
people, stands before them, precedes them, and follows
them.

Significantly, in the assembly's liturgical space, there is
a special place for the book of the Scriptures: the ambo.

----

*verbum*" ("The word is added to the [material] element, and there
results the Sacrament, as if itself also a kind of visible word": St.
Augustine, *Homilies on the Gospel of John*, 80.3, trans. John Gibb
and James Innes, Nicene and Post-Nicene Fathers 7 [Grand Rapids,
MI: Eerdmans, repr. 1991], 344).

15. On this schema of four characteristics, Louis-Marie Chauvet,
*Symbol and Sacrament: Sacramental Reinterpretation of Christian
Existence*, trans. Madeleine M. Beaumont and Patrick Madigan
(Collegeville, MN: Liturgical Press, 1994), 210.

The book is not held in the hands of the lector, because it does not belong to the lector. Rather, it is placed on the ambo to signify that the Word of God, of which the Scriptures are the *sacramentum*, precedes the convocation and remains there even when the assembly disperses. The proclamation of the Scriptures to an assembly is a sending forth of the Word of God that creates of them a community of believers. The Liturgy of the Word is an event in which God speaks to his people, thereby creating a relationship that forms, molds, and creates the community.

The liturgical assembly is the foundational hermeneutical location of the Scriptures; they are heard and understood fully in the *ekklesía* because the liturgical assembly is where they are born. Exegesis recognizes and takes into account that the *qahal*, the liturgical assembly of Israel, was the decisive (though not exclusive) place of the progressive formation of the Hebrew Scriptures. In turn, the *ekklesía*, the Christian assembly, represents the privileged space where the first Christians reread the Old Testament in light of the coming of Jesus of Nazareth. For this reason, we are able to fully realize today the decisive role that liturgical praxis has played in the reception and the transmission of biblical texts and how liturgical use was one of the primary criteria in the formation of the canon of Scripture, first Hebrew and then Christian: "The canonical writings are those that receive authority through public reading,"[16] as Paul Beauchamp has effectively summarized the matter.

To recognize that the assembly is the foundational hermeneutical location of the Scriptures means also to see that the word of God contained in the Scriptures is fully understood only in the context of the assembly. One of the

---

16. Cf. Paul Beauchamp, *L'uno e l'altro Testamento: Saggio di lettura* (Brescia, Paideia, 1985), 219.

Western church's greatest preachers and commentators on the Scriptures, Pope Gregory the Great, recognized that his understanding and discernment of the Scriptures was fully operative only in the midst of his community. In an often noted passage of one of the homilies on the book of the prophet Ezekiel, he says:

> Perhaps some of you are reproaching me in your hearts, that I presume to explain such great mysteries of the prophet Ezekiel from which great commentators have shied away. Please know the attitude with which I do this—not recklessly, but with humility. I know, in fact, that there are many things about the Scriptures that I have been unable to understand on my own; I have understood them only when standing before my brothers. . . . It is clear, in fact, that this [understanding] is granted to me thanks to the merits of those around me. . . . The meaning grows and pride diminishes when I know that it is through you that I am learning what I teach when I stand before you. It is the truth—much of what I say to you I listen to with you.[17]

Gregory the Great recognizes that personal meditation on the Scriptures, *lectio divina*, is not enough to understand them fully; when one hears them in the company of one's brothers and sisters in faith, then the meaning of the Scriptures grows more clear. For Gregory, the assembly is the theological *locus* of hearing the Word, understanding it, interpreting it, actualizing it, and allowing it to become effective.

Knowing that the structure and dynamic of the liturgical assembly establishes the structure and dynamic of ecclesial life also means recognizing that in every Christian com-

17. Gregory the Great, *Homilies on Ezekiel* 2.2.1. [My translation from the Italian.—Trans.]

munity, no matter how small or poor, the fullest and most authentic hearing and understanding of the word of God happens only "when standing before [one's] brothers [and sisters]," that is, in the context of the liturgical assembly. The fact that the assembly forms the life of a Christian community means the communal hearing of the word of God cannot be limited exclusively to the moment of liturgy. Just as the entire community hears the word of God during the liturgy and interprets the word that it hears, so all aspects of ecclesial life must include communal interpretation of the word of God.

Every session of the Second Vatican Council began with the enthronement of the Book of the Gospels. This gesture expressed the conciliar assembly's openness and submission to God's word, and its desire to place its work and deliberations under the primacy of the Gospel. In the same way, when a Christian community confronts a problem or makes a decision central to its life together, it must consider the question in light of the word of God, allowing the Gospel to guide the situation and inspire the right decision. Just as the entire community, in the liturgical assembly, hears and interprets the Scriptures, so all the members must be involved in discerning the good of the community.

"This [understanding] is granted to me thanks to the merits of those around me." Pope Gregory's statement suggests that *authentic understanding is by its very nature an act of communion*. This means that every Christian community must learn that evangelical discernment is always the fruit of a common, never individual, understanding. To affirm this means recognizing that understanding is the fruit of *koinonia*, and at the same time that *koinonia* is the result of a common understanding. This seems to be the meaning of the words of Gregory the Great, "There are many things about the Scriptures that I have been unable to understand on my own; I have understood them only when standing before my brothers." The word of God is a word of communion, and only in communion is full understanding truly found.

## God Enters into a Covenant with His People

In the Sinai assembly, the covenant was sealed with a sacrifice: "Moses took the blood and dashed it on the people, and said, 'See the blood of the covenant that the LORD has made with you in accordance with all these words'" (Exod 24:8). God, who called Israel and revealed to it his Word, now seals the covenant with his people with a sign. When Christians gather in eucharistic assembly, they must be constantly aware of living Israel's experience of escape from Egypt, of repeating what was done by the assembly of Sinai, the "church of the desert."

Jesus of Nazareth's entire existence was directed toward renewing the covenant of Sinai. His entire life was *ekklesía*, the fulfillment of that "holy gathering" initiated by God with Israel. Jesus' entire human journey was formed by the structure and dynamic of the covenant: he called the new people of God by calling the Twelve to follow him. He gave them his Word and sealed the new and eternal covenant in his blood, not by chance with words that reflect those of Moses: "This cup that is poured out for you is the new covenant in my blood" (Luke 22:20). Through the coming of his Son, God calls and gathers his people anew and so forms the church of messianic times. "[I]t is better for you to have one man die for the people" (John 11:50); the evangelist John interprets these words of the high priest Caiaphas as a prophecy, and he comments: "being high priest that year [Caiaphas] prophesied that Jesus was about to die for the nation, and not for the nation only, but to gather into one the dispersed children on God" (John

11:51-52). Before the contradictions of the universal vocation of the Jewish assembly, Jesus abolishes all the proscriptions and prohibitions that put limits on the calling together of humanity in assembly. He opens access to the assembly of the believers to the blind, the lame, children, public sinners, publicans. This seems to be what the evangelist Matthew is expressing when he suggests a close link between the many healings worked at the lake and the second multiplication of the loaves, which we know includes strong eucharistic connotations. The evangelist chooses words to describe the crowd gathered around Jesus as a true and proper gathering: "Great crowds came to him, bringing with them the lame, the maimed, the blind, the mute, and many others. They put them at his feet, and he cured them" (Matt 15:30).

According to the Gospel of Mark, Jesus calls together in assembly not only the children of Israel but also the pagans. In fact, while for Mark the first multiplication of loaves happens on Israelite soil and the crowd is composed of Jews, the second multiplication of loaves happens in pagan territory ("in the region of the Decapolis" [Mark 7:31]) and the crowds that "come from a great distance" (Mark 8:3) are pagans. While in the first multiplication they collected twelve baskets of bread for the twelve tribes of Israel, in the second they collected seven baskets for the seven pagan nations, according to the number indicated in Genesis 10.

In Christ, all people are called to become the people of God. In him, Jews and pagans together constitute the "holy gathering" called and nourished by the "one bread" in order to be "one body" (cf. 1 Cor 10:17). Christ is therefore the true *qahal* willed by God, and the people of the new covenant, the church, is his body: "[God] has made him the head over all things for the church, which is his body"

(Eph 1:22-23). The *ekklesía* is the body of Christ, but at the same time the body of Christ is *ekklesía*, the convocation formed by that "great multitude that no one could count, from every nation, from all tribes and peoples and languages" (Rev 7:9).

We might say, then, that Christology is actually a theology of assembly, and that when the author of the Letter to the Hebrews puts on the lips of Jesus the words of Psalm 40—"Sacrifices and offerings you have not desired, / but a body you have prepared for me" (Heb 10:5)—the reference is not only to the historical body of Jesus but the body that is the church, the people God has gathered through him. To discern in the *ekklesía* the body of the Son means to recognize the fulfillment of the Targum to Psalm 45:11. That verse reads, "Hear, O daughter, consider and incline your ear." The Targum, a liturgical interpretation of the Hebrew Scriptures rooted in synagogue worship, interprets that passage with the words, "Hear the Law of his mouth, O Assembly of Israel, and see his wonderful works; and you shall incline your ears to the words of the Law."[18] While the Targum interprets the bride in Psalm 45 as the assembly of the children of Israel called to the wedding with the messiah king, the Christian interpretation of this psalm sees the celebration of the wedding of God's anointed one, the Christ, with the bride-church gathered from among all the peoples.

Since the day of Pentecost, the work of the Holy Spirit has been to continue Christ's mission of gathering the dispersed children of God, giving life to the people of the new covenant. It is no coincidence that a theology of eucharistic assembly was reborn in the Catholic Church at the same

18. *The Targum of Psalms* 45:11, trans. David M. Stec (Collegeville, MN: Liturgical Press, 2004), 96–97.

time Catholic theology was rediscovering the close connections between the Holy Spirit and the Eucharist. The end and purpose to which Christians are called in assembly is the body of Christ. The transformation of bread and wine into the body and blood of Christ by the action of the holy Spirit is not, in fact, an end in itself; rather, the gifts are transformed so that those who eat them may become what they receive. This is the dynamic of the two epicleses of the eucharistic prayer: one epiclesis over the gifts and a second over the communicants. For example, in the epiclesis over the communicants of Eucharistic Prayer II of the *Roman Missal*, the church prays:

> Humbly we pray
> that, partaking of the Body and Blood of Christ,
> we may be gathered into one by the Holy Spirit.[19]

There are two bodies placed in relationship here: the eucharistic body and the ecclesial body. The former finds its goal in the latter. The proper end of the eucharistic body is to form the ecclesial body. In this dynamic, the Holy Spirit always continues gathering into one body the scattered children of God. The church cannot be satisfied with having the Eucharist; it does not possess it. The Eucharist serves no purpose if it remains simply an object to be possessed and adored. The church, however, is called to become the eucharistic body of the Lord; the truth of the eucharistic body is the ecclesial body.

Augustine expressed this dynamic in some of his homilies to the neophytes, and his comments truly represent the high point of Western eucharistic theology. Augustine preached:

19. *The Roman Missal, Third Edition* (Collegeville, MN: Liturgical Press, 2011), 648.

[I]f you want to understand the [mystery of the] body of Christ, listen to the apostle telling the faithful, 'You, though, are the body of Christ and its members' (1 Cor 12:27). So if it's you that are the body of Christ and its members, it's the mystery meaning you that has been placed on the Lord's table; what you receive is the mystery that means you. It is to what you are that you reply 'Amen,' and by replying you express your assent. What you hear, you see, is the body of Christ, and you answer 'Amen.' So be a member of the body of Christ in order to make that 'Amen' true. . . . Be what you can see and receive what you are.[20]

In another homily he says: "What you receive is what you yourselves are, thanks to the grace by which you have been redeemed."[21] And again: "Believers know the body of Christ, if they do not neglect to be the body of Christ."[22]

To become what we receive—this is the *mandatum eucharisticum*, the "eucharistic commandment." For this reason, the expression *communion* does not refer solely to the act of *eating* the eucharistic bread but also to the reason, the *purpose* for which Christians eat it: to be church-communion, to become one body in Christ. John of Damascus writes: "Communion [*koinonia*] is spoken of, and it is an actual communion, because through it we have communion with Christ and share in His flesh and His divinity; through it, we have communion and are united with one another."[23]

---

20. St. Augustine, Sermon 272, in *Sermons*, part 3, vol. 7, trans. Edmund Hill (New Rochelle, NY: New City Press, 1993), 300–301.

21. St. Augustine, Sermon 229A, in *Sermons*, part 3, vol. 6, trans. Edmund Hill (New Rochelle, NY: New City Press, 1993), 270.

22. Ibid., *Homilies on the Gospel of John*, XXVI, 13, trans. John Gibb and James Innes, Nicene and Post-Nicene Fathers 7 (Grand Rapids, MI: Eerdmans, 1991), 172.

23. John of Damascus, *Exposition of the Orthodox Faith*, XIII, trans. S.D.F. Salmond, Nicene and Post-Nicene Fathers 9 (Grand Rapids, MI: Eerdmans, 1983), 84.

To *receive* communion is to *be* a communion. This truth is expressed well in Eucharistic Prayer II for Masses with Children, by the acclamation that is repeated during the intercessions of that prayer: "One body, one spirit to your glory, Lord!"[24] While this anaphora is a fine illustration, the same might be said of every eucharistic prayer: in the section of intercessions, the assembly calls on the Lord to grant unity to the church, asking to be made one body and one spirit to the glory of God. The assembly asks the Lord, "Make us one body!" or "Make us one in Christ!" The frequent repetition of invocations like these can help to nourish an authentic awareness among the people of the nature of both the Eucharist and the church. In this way, the liturgy can profoundly form the faith and the life of the church.

When Christians understand that the purpose of the Eucharist is to make them one body, a communion of brothers and sisters in faith, they will no longer view their participation in the Sunday liturgical assembly as a matter of precept or formal obligation but rather as expressing their very identity. They will see their presence at the Sunday liturgy as an essential part of calling themselves Christian.

24. [The *editio typica* of Eucharistic Prayer II for Masses with Children includes the acclamation, *"Unum corpus, unus spiritus sint ad gloriam tuam, Domine"* (*Missale Romanum*, Editio Typica Tertia [Vatican City: Libreria Editrice Vaticana, 2002], 1281), which would be, in English, "One body, one spirit to your glory, Lord." The Italian edition of the Missal, to which the author refers, translates it similarly: *"Un cuor solo, un'anima sola, per la tua gloria, Signore!"* However, the approved ICEL translation of this prayer published in connection with the third edition of the *Roman Missal* (though not in the Missal itself) ignores this acclamation and provides a different one in its place: "We praise you, we bless you, we thank you" (*Eucharistic Prayers for Masses with Children* [Washington, DC: United States Conference of Catholic Bishops, 2011], 13–14).—Trans.]

Augustine provides a good illustration of the impossibility of calling oneself a Christian without being part of the church of Christ or joining its Sunday assembly when he reports in his *Confessions* the dialogue between the bishop Simplicianus and the noted Roman rhetorician Marius Victorinus, who converted to Christianity around 355:

> Victorinus was in the habit of reading holy scripture and intensively studying all the Christian writings, which he subjected to close scrutiny; and he would say to Simplicianus, not openly, but in private, intimate conversation, "I am already a Christian, you know." But the other always replied, "I will not believe that, nor count you among Christians, until I see you in Christ's church." Victorinus would chaff him: "It's the walls that make Christians, then?". . . [S]uddenly and without warning he said to Simplicianus, who told this tale, "Let us go to church: I want to become Christian."[25]

The close relationship between the *ekklesía* and Christian identity is the reason for the repeated demand we find in some of the most ancient canonical-liturgical documents that Christians not abandon the eucharistic assembly. In the *Apostolic Constitutions*, which dates to the fourth century in its original Syriac, we read:

> In your teaching, O bishop, command and exhort the people to come constantly to church, morning and evening every day, and by no means to forsake it on any account, but to assemble together without ceasing, that they may not mutilate the Church by withdrawing themselves [from the assembly], and [so] amputating a member from the body of Christ. For these are words which

---

25. St. Augustine, *The Confessions* 8.4, trans. Maria Boulding (Hyde Park, NY: New City Press, 1997), 187–88.

concern not only the priests but also the laity, each of whom, if he reflects upon them, must understand that what the Lord has said applies to himself: 'He that is not with me is against me, and he who does not gather with me scatters.' Since you are the members of Christ, do not scatter yourselves by not assembling together; since you have Christ as your Head, according to his promise, meeting together with you and united [himself] with you, do not neglect yourselves, do not deprive the Saviour of his own members, do not divide his body, do not scatter his members, and do not prefer the business of this world to the word of God; but assemble yourselves together every day, morning and evening, singing and praying in the house of the Lord, saying in the morning the sixty-second psalm, and in the evening the one hundred and fortieth. Above all, on the sabbath day and on Sunday, the day of the resurrection of the Lord, be even more diligent to assemble together, sending up praise to God who created all things through Jesus, and sent him to us, and allowed him to suffer [for us], and raised him from the dead. For how will he justify himself before God, who does not join the assembly on that day to hear the saving word of the resurrection?[26]

Another Syriac text, this one with origins in the third century, the *Didascalia Apostolorum,* includes this exhortation to the bishop:

When you are teaching you are to command and exhort the people that they should gather in church, and come together always, that none should be absent and so reduce the church through their withdrawal, so as to make the

26. *Apostolic Constitutions*, 2.59, in *The Liturgical Portions of the Apostolic Constitutions: A Text for Students*, trans. W. Jardine Grisbrooke, Grove Liturgical Study 61 (Bramcote, UK: Grove Books, 1990), 53–54.

body of Christ defective in a limb. People should not simply be thinking of others, but of themselves, since it is said, "Whoever does not gather with me, is a scatterer." Since you are members of Christ you should not scatter yourselves from the church by failing to gather with others.[27]

These texts demonstrate that for the ancient church, participation in the assembly was not considered simply the observance of a precept but rather a Christological and ecclesiological action. The church's commandment that Christians not abandon the Sunday assembly is intended to remind us of an interior obligation that comes from faith. One cannot be Christian without participating in the assembly of the church. This is a matter of identity, both of the church and of the individual Christian.

"Do not neglect yourselves, do not deprive the Saviour of his own members, do not divide his body, do not scatter his members." The body-church must become the greatest likeness of Jesus himself. The life of the church must be the very life of Jesus.

## The Assembly, the Place Where the Spirit Flourishes

The conviction that the structure and dynamic of ecclesial life reflects the structure and dynamic of the assembly helps us understand that the church either is communion or it is not the body of Christ. If it has not become that which it receives, to use Augustine's words, the church has not achieved it purpose. The *Apostolic Tra-*

---

27. "The Didascalia Apostolorum, 13," in *The Didascalia Apostolorum: An English Version*, trans. Alistair Stewart-Sykes (Turnhout, Belgium: Brepols, 2009), 178.

*dition*, a canonical-liturgical document dated around 215, defines the liturgical assembly as the place *"ubi floret Spiritus"*: "Let [the faithful] hasten to the church, where the spirit flourishes."[28] The assembly is the place where the Holy Spirit "bears fruit."[29] It is the epiphany of all the gifts that the Spirit gives to the church. In it are gathered all the components of the church. Each member should be present, because this gathering of the gifts of the Spirit is found only and uniquely in the gathering of the members of the community.

Liturgical praxis must become ecclesial praxis. Just as no one in the liturgical assembly does everything but each one acts according to his own role, so in the daily life of the Christian community, no one can do everything, but everyone is called to collaborate to build up the church according to his or her gifts and ministries.

In the assembly the presbyter is the *proestós*, the one who stands before the assembly to preside over it and to guide it; but he is at the same time an integral part of the assembly, neither above it nor outside of it but within it. The presbyter, like Moses, calls the people together in the name of God. In his daily exercise of the ministry of the Word, he makes the word of God, which speaks to the

---

28. *The Apostolic Tradition*, 35, trans. Paul F. Bradshaw, Maxwell E. Johnson, and L. Edward Phillips (Minneapolis: Fortress, 2002), 178.

29. Where Bernard Botte's critical edition here translates the Sahidic version into Latin with *floret*, he translates the Arabic and Ethiopic versions with *fructificat*. Regarding the choice of *fructificat*, Botte comments, "The expression is easily understandable if one considers that *pneûma* in the *Tradition* refers not only to the person of the Holy Spirit, but also to charisms" (B. Botte, *La Tradition apostolique de saint Hippolyte. Essai de reconstitution* [Munster: Aschendorff, 1989], 83n2).

heart of every believer, resound in the community and challenge each Christian interiorly, calling him to encounter the Lord and the sisters and brothers in faith.[30] Like Moses, the presbyter carries out the ministry of the Word by breaking the bread of the Word, interpreting the Scriptures before the community. Like Moses, he leads the people's prayer, acting as intercessor on behalf of the people before God and on behalf of God before the people. At the same time, the presbyter is called to preside over the community by coordinating the gifts of the Spirit in the conviction that no one possesses all, few possess many, but all possess at least one, as the Apostle writes: "To each is given the manifestation of the Spirit for the common good" (1 Cor 12:7). Just as the presbyter is, in the liturgical assembly, the guarantor of communion with the local church and through it with the universal church (and therefore it is through him that the community receives the eucharistic body), so in the daily life of the church, the presbyter must be the guarantor of communion in the Christian community, in a constant and never-ending process of understanding better how each component contributes to that communion.

Communion is learned and continually perfected. More than any other aspect of ecclesial life, the liturgical assembly is the home and the school of communion. The structure and the dynamic of the liturgical assembly will have truly succeeded in shaping the concrete and ordinary life of the church when not only the liturgy is eucharistic, but the

---

30. The conciliar decree *Presbyterorum Ordinis* indicates the link between the exercise of the "sacred task of the gospel" on the part of priests and the liturgical convocation, affirming that "it is by the apostolic herald of the Gospel that the People of God is called together and gathered" (n. 2).

structures and dynamics of the church are also eucharistic. Communion must "happen" not only in the liturgy but also in the daily life of the Christian community. Consequently, what happens in the eucharistic assembly must not be considered a reality that is parallel to ecclesial life but identical to it. Liturgical praxis and ecclesial praxis must come together to assume the same dynamic and the same goal.

With respect to both its own nature and its relationship to the world, either the church *is* communion or it is *not* the body of Christ. The community of the disciples of Christ is his body when it is, for the world, a sign of communion. In the Eucharistic Prayer for Use in Masses for Various Needs, we ask the Lord,

> that in a world torn by strife
> your people may shine forth
> as a prophetic sign of unity and concord.[31]

This text is an eloquent example of how the law of prayer must become the church's law of living. We must build a Christian community that is a prophetic sign of unity in the midst of the divisions of the world and a prophetic sign of peace in the midst of wars and conflicts. In the same anaphora, we pray,

> [M]ay your Church stand as a living witness
> to truth and freedom,
> to peace and justice,
> that all people may be raised up to a new hope.[32]

When people see in the Christian community a concrete praxis of communion and they discern in it a place of

---

31. *The Roman Missal*, 779.
32. Ibid., 796.

mercy and justice, where love is the supreme law, then we will truly be witnesses, even without words, that love is stronger than death and that death no longer has power over life. It will only be then that people will be able to say of the church in its journey through history what Peter says, in the Acts of the Apostles, about Jesus: "he went about doing good and healing all who were oppressed by the devil, for God was with him" (Acts 10:38).

To truly understand what it means for the liturgical assembly to form the life of the church is to extend to the eucharistic assembly what Irenaeus of Lyons said succinctly about the Eucharist: "Our way of thinking accords with the Eucharist, and the Eucharist confirms our way of thinking."[33] Yes, our way of thinking and acting as church must accord with the eucharistic assembly, and the eucharistic assembly should confirm our way of thinking and acting as church.

---

33. Irenaeus of Lyons, *Against the Heresies* 4.18.5. [My translation from the Italian.—Trans.]

# Chapter Six

# Presbyters Formed by the Liturgy

*"[E]ven the shepherds themselves are sheep."*
—Augustine of Hippo[1]

## *The Liturgy, First School of Liturgy*

The meaning of the liturgy is understood first of all through consideration of the praxis of the liturgy, and so the first and fundamental school of liturgy is the liturgy itself.[2] I reflect in this chapter on the role of the liturgy in

1. St. Augustine, Tractate 123, *Tractates on the Gospel of John 112–24*, The Fathers of the Church 92, trans. John W. Rettig (Washington, DC: Catholic University of America Press, 1995), 81.

2. This chapter was originally published as "Presbiteri formati dalla liturgia," *Rivista del Clero* 88, no. 3 (2007): 193–202. For more on the theme of the liturgical formation of presbyters, see also A. M. Triacca, "Presbyter: Spiritus Sancti vas.' 'Modelli' di presbitero testimoniati dall'eucologia (Approcio metodologico alla 'ex orandi' in vista della 'lex vivendi')," in *La formazione al sacerdozio minsteriale nella catechesis e nella testimonianza di vita dei Padri. Convegno di studio e aggiornamento*, ed. S. Felici (Rome: LAS, 1992), 193–236.

the liturgical formation of ordained ministers, though I hasten to acknowledge that the liturgy is by itself inadequate for such formation. Other means are necessary, particularly the study of history and liturgical theology during the years of formation for pastoral ministry and then continuing through the course of one's ministry in an ongoing way. For brevity and clarity, we will refer here to presbyters in particular, though it is surely true that bishops, presbyters and deacons are each formed by the liturgy in a distinct way, thanks to the unique features of their own ministries.

We begin by noting what has been frequently noted by many observers in recent years—that is, the urgency of recovering the centrality of the liturgy in the life of the Western church. In the document that presented its pastoral priorities for the first decade of the new millennium, the Italian bishops conference observed, "In spite of the extraordinary benefits brought about by the liturgical reform of the Second Vatican Council, one of the most difficult problems today is the transmission of the true meaning of the Christian liturgy. . . . It seems at times that the meaning of the sacramental event is forgotten."[3] While this evaluation certainly concerns every member of the church, it is especially important to presbyters who must be the first to understand and to transmit the true meaning of the Christian liturgy.

Along these same lines, Cardinal Dionigi Tettamanzi, the archbishop of Milan, has insisted, in a book on the spiritual life of the presbyter, on the necessity of "reestablishing the centrality of the liturgy."[4] Tettamanzi writes:

---

3. Conferenza Episcopale Italiana, *Comunicare il Vangelo in un Mondo che Cambia* (Bologna: EDB, 2001), n. 49.

4. Dionigi Tettamanzi, *La Vita Spirituale del Prete* (Casale Monferrato: Piemme, 2002), 36.

"We must acknowledge the reality, even in the lives of priests, of a certain disconnect or interruption between the true meaning of the liturgical celebration and the exercise of the pastoral ministry."[5] The same point is made by Enzo Bianchi, who writes, "Perhaps the time has not yet come for a true reestablishment of liturgy at the center of the life of the presbyter. But I often have the impression of there being today a deep divide between ministry and liturgy."[6]

"Disconnect," "interruption," "divide"—they are synonyms used by these authors to describe the current state of the relationship between liturgy and presbyters. In light of this situation, I suggest three important places where the liturgy might play a greater role in the liturgical formation of presbyters: the liturgy forms the presbyter for liturgical prayer; the liturgy forms the presbyter for liturgical presiding; the liturgy forms the presbyter for mystagogy.

## The Liturgy Forms the Presbyter for Liturgical Prayer

A poor relationship between liturgy and prayer is disastrous not only to both our liturgy and our personal prayer but also to Christian living in general. We are therefore compelled to ask some questions: When Christians today—including presbyters among them—think about prayer, do they think about liturgy first of all? Where and how are believers formed in their prayer today? Is the liturgy truly lived today as the first and fundamental experience of prayer? Although there is and certainly should be more to the prayer life of Christians—and therefore of presbyters—

---

5. Ibid., 38.
6. Enzo Bianchi, *Ai presbiteri* (Bose: Qiqajon, 2004), 45.

than the liturgy, it is easy to get the impression that those who regularly practice and enjoy periods of solitary and silent prayer, or who participate in free-flowing and fervent prayer within small groups, are often the very same people who approach the liturgy with the greatest dissatisfaction and discomfort. They are the ones who readily admit to having no understanding of the liturgical prayers and to experiencing the liturgy as cold, formal, and difficult. These Christians, among both laity and presbyters, recognize that the liturgy is not their fundamental experience of prayer, thus perpetuating the disconnect between liturgy and prayer that first the liturgical movement and then the liturgical reform intended more than anything else to overcome. Even in 1959, the desire to bring the people of God back to the prayer of the church met with resistance and opposition, as was seen in the objections to the principle insights of the liturgical movement voiced by Jacques and Raisa Maritain. The two openly admitted to feeling threatened in their most intimate religious convictions by the work of certain liturgists who, with the best of intentions, endeavored to bring the people back to the prayer of the church.[7]

The connections between liturgy and prayer in the life of the church will never be made unless they are made first of all in the spiritual lives of the church's presbyters. The spiritual life of the presbyter must be the place where liturgy and prayer encounter one another again, the place where the objectivity of the liturgy and the subjectivity of the individual meet, are formed, combine to form a single reality, and at times may even, inevitably, oppose and collide with one another. This raises the question: Can we say

---

7. Cf. Jacques and Raisa Maritain, *Liturgie et Contemplation* (Paris: DDB, 1959).

that the Liturgy of the Hours (and in particular the praying of the psalms) and the euchology of the Missal (and in particular the eucharistic prayer and the collects) are, for Christians today and for presbyters in particular, the source and norm of their prayer?

By way of example, let us consider the praying of the psalms. The psalter has been, from the beginning, the school of Christian prayer *par excellence*. It is not by chance that every liturgy begins with a psalm, either invitatory or introit, as if to say that the church's prayer begins in the psalter. From the daily, even hourly, praying of the psalms, the presbyter learns to pray by attending to the difficult art of hearing the word of God, of interiorizing and interpreting it. Psalmody forces oneself, for example, to confront the difficulty of the prayer and the sense of impotence that the psalms sometimes present. Dietrich Bonhoeffer wrote, "A psalm that we cannot utter as a prayer, that makes us falter and horrifies us, is a hint to us that here Someone else is praying, not we; that the One who is here protesting his innocence, who is invoking God's judgment, who has come to such infinite depths of suffering, is none other than Jesus Christ himself."[8]

In the canonical obligation of presbyters to pray the Liturgy of the Hours, we can discern the wisdom of the church that liturgical prayer might form and shape their prayer, hour after hour, day after day, leading eventually to full maturity in the prayer of the church—maturity in content and form, in style and expression. Martin Luther wrote: "Those who begin to pray the psalter in a serious

---

8. Dietrich Bonhoeffer, *Life Together*, trans. John W. Doberstein (New York: Harper and Row, 1954), 45.

and regular way will soon abandon the other easy, particular, and pious little prayers."[9]

We therefore must pose this question, hesitantly but also frankly: Why, fifty years after the start of the conciliar liturgical reform, is the Liturgy of the Hours still not yet the prayer of all the people of God? Why in the ordinary praxis of the Christian community has a healthy balance between the frequency of celebration of the Eucharist and of the Liturgy of the Hours eluded us? Is this long exile of the praying of the psalms by the people of God perhaps caused in part by the fact that the presbyters still struggle to pray the psalms, that psalmody is not for them really prayer?

One principle of liturgical prayer is this: the person who learns to pray the hymns and psalms, the collects and anaphoras, learns the grammar and syntax of the prayer of the church. Formed by the liturgy, the presbyter learns that liturgical prayer is above all *true*, in the sense suggested by Romano Guardini, who wrote:

> [A] prayer which is intended for everyday use of a large body of people must be restrained. If, therefore, it has uncontrolled and unbalanced emotion for a foundation, it is doubly dangerous. It will operate in one of two ways. Either the people who use it will take it seriously, and probably will then feel obliged to force themselves into acquiescence with an emotion that they have never, generally speaking, experienced, or which, at any rate, they are not experiencing at that particular moment, thus perverting or degrading the religious feeling. Or else indifference, if they are of a phlegmatic temperament, will come to their

---

9. Cited in Dietrich Bonhoeffer, *Pregare i Salmi con Cristo* (Brescia: Queriniana, 1969), 77.

aid; they then take the phrases at less than their face value, and consequently the word is depreciated.[10]

The liturgy, then, forms the presbyter for a kind of liturgical prayer that is *simple* and *clear*. Simple prayer is understandable even to those who are simple. Liturgical prayer does not aspire to seem more intelligent than the God to whom it is addressed. The liturgy offers prayer that is *sober* and *fundamental*. Glosses to the euchological texts offered by presiders rarely add anything that is truly necessary; the result is most often lost momentum in the prayer itself and confusion among those who hear it prayed. The liturgy, furthermore, forms the presbyter for liturgical prayer that is *intense*, *strong*, and fundamentally *positive*, prayer that avoids the hesitancy of "if" or "but," without ever being brusque. Finally it teaches a prayer marked by *respect* for God and for others, in that it is always directed to God.

Personal expression and freedom on the part of the presbyter in proclaiming the prayer comes into play through his thorough understanding of the liturgy. This alone is the source of the authentic spontaneity and prudent creativity that a presbyter will need to provide the necessary interventions that liturgical presiding sometimes calls for and that he must be able to offer, since the Missal cannot anticipate everything: admonitions, short introductions, brief glosses, intercessory prayers, adequate formulas in particular circumstances. The ritual, in fact, does not exhaust the rite.

Finally, the presbyter formed in the school of liturgical prayer will speak to people about God as the liturgy speaks

---

10. Romano Guardini, *The Spirit of the Liturgy*, trans. Ada Lane (London: Sheed and Ward, 1930), 19.

of God. He will have learned to evangelize from praying in the liturgy, because the presider announces the gospel in the prayers he proclaims.

## The Liturgy Forms the Presbyter for Liturgical Presiding

The most recent studies on liturgical presiding identify the emergence of a new moment in the ministry of presiding, a development that Louis-Marie Chauvet has described as "liturgical presiding in search of a new ethos."[11] While there was a time, before the conciliar reform, when the presbyter simply carried out the role of "officiant" in the liturgy, and it was enough that he correctly follow the rigid instructions prescribed for the ritual, today the situation is different. The constant, excessive, and therefore problematic face-to-face relationship that now marks the dynamic between presider and people has profoundly changed and conditioned this relationship. Added to this are the crises of authority and institution that have marked our society in recent decades, sparing neither the church nor the presbyter in his roles as leader of the Christian community and, in particular, as presider at liturgy. For this reason, the authority of the presbyter is no longer legitimized simply by the "spiritual power" conferred on him by the sacrament of orders. Rather, this authority is "received" by the faithful only if the priest shows an effective competence combined with a certain personal charisma. In other words, the spiri-

---

11. Louis-Marie Chauvet, "La présidence liturgique en quête d'un nouvel 'ethos,'" *La Maison-Dieu* 230 (2002): 43–66. Chauvet later published an expanded version of this study in J. Lamberts, ed., *"Ars Celebrandi": The Art to Celebrate the Liturgy* (Leuven: Peeters, 2002), 49–64.

tual authority *given* by the sacrament of orders must be accompanied at the same time by an *acquired* authority.

The search for this new ethos calls for changes in the way we understand the *ars celebrandi*. We can limit ourselves here to consideration of one in particular: in the new ethos of liturgical presiding, the presbyter is called to help the assembly make the prayer of the church its own. He is prepared for this task by the liturgy itself, in the sense that the liturgy puts the presbyter simultaneously within the liturgical assembly and at the head of it. He is before all else a Christian among Christians, because baptism precedes the sacrament of orders, by which the presbyter stands before the assembly *in nomine Christi*, and is both its foundation and condition. In his exercise of the role of liturgical presider, the presbyter is constantly called to live this unique and challenging dual role. *With* the assembly he confesses his sin, saying, "I confess to almighty God"; *for* the assembly he invokes mercy: "May almighty God have mercy on us . . ." *With* the assembly he hears the word of God addressed to him; *for* the assembly he is the proclaimer and interpreter of the Word. *With* the assembly he confesses, "I believe in God"; speaking *to* the assembly, he asks, "Do you believe in God?" Augustine, commenting on Jesus' command to Peter to feed his flock, says, "[T]he shepherds themselves are sheep" (*pastores ipsi sunt oves*).[12] And elsewhere he says, "You are his sheep and we are sheep with you because we are Christians . . . We shepherd you and we are shepherded with you" (*pascimus vos, pascimur vobiscum*),[13] or translated literally, "We provide your nourishment and with you we are nourished."

---

12. St. Augustine, Tractate 123.

13. Ibid., *Sermones in Bibliotheca Casinensi editi* I, 133, 5.13, in *Miscellanea agostiniana. Testi e studi*, I. *Sancti Augustini Sermones post Maurinos reperti*, ed. the monastic hermits of St. Augustine

"*Pascimus vos*," "we provide your nourishment": presiding over the assembly *in nomine Christi et in nomine ecclesiae*, the presbyter is called to make the community's prayer one with the prayer of the church. But "*pascimur vobiscum*," "with you we are nourished": inasmuch as he is Christian, the presbyter is called when he presides over the assembly to pray the words he says, because the most efficacious way for the presbyter to help the assembly make its prayer one with the prayer of the church is first of all to interiorize it himself. When the presbyter presides at liturgy, he presides over the *ecclesia orans*; in that moment he is at the service of the church at prayer, making himself servant of the prayer of all the faithful.

Pope Benedict XVI, speaking to presbyters of the *ars celebrandi*, insisted on the necessity of "enter[ing] with our *mens* into the *vox* of the Church." He continued:

> To the extent that we have interiorized this structure, comprehended this structure, assimilated the words of the Liturgy, we can enter into this inner consonance and thus not only speak to God as individuals, but enter into the "we" of the Church, which is praying. And we thus transform our "I" in this way, by entering into the "we" of the Church, enriching and enlarging this "I," praying with the Church, with the words of the Church, truly being in conversation with God.[14]

(Rome: Typis polyglottis vaticanis, 1930), 404, 410. [My translation from the Italian.—Trans.]
    14. "Meeting of His Holiness Benedict XVI with the Priests of the Diocese of Albano," 31 August 2006: http://www.vatican.va /holy_father/benedict_xvi/speeches/2006/august/documents/hf_ben -xvi_spe_20060831_sacerdoti-albano_en.html, accessed November 24, 2013.

From the presbyter's "I" to the church's "we"—this is the formative action of the liturgy, preparing the presbyter to preside over the prayer of the church. The presbyter, then, needs to be not only a person of prayer—this is the call of every Christian. The presbyter must also be able to preside over the prayer of the church, to be the servant of the *ecclesia orans*. This means more than simply "getting an assembly to pray"; it means leading an assembly in prayer by means of the prayer of the church. Only the presbyter who has personally interiorized the church's liturgical prayer will be able to encourage the same interiorization by the assembly. This is the meaning of the admonition of Isaac of Nineveh, who taught in the middle of the seventh century: "In the verses of your song and of your prayer, take care not to be a conductor of words coming from someone else. . . . Pray those words as your own, beseeching, with discernment . . . as one who is aware of the true essence of what he is doing."[15]

To pray while one presides over an assembly is not a simple matter; it is the fruit of a constant process of interiorization, assimilation, and therefore spiritual understanding of liturgical prayer. This is the meaning of the Benedictine adage, *"mens concordat voci"* [let our minds coincide with our voices], where the priority belongs to the voice, to the words we say, while the *mens*, the mind and spirit, must be aligned to the liturgical text, interiorizing what is external. When the presbyter assimilates liturgical prayer, the liturgy itself forms him and makes him better able to preside, to be the servant of the church's prayer, and therefore to unite the assembly to Christ's prayer to the Father.

15. Isaac of Nineveh, *Prima collezione* 53, in Id., *Un'umile speranza. Antologia*, S. Chiala, ed. (Bose: Qiqajon, 1999), 160. [My translation from the Italian.—Trans.]

## The Liturgy Forms the Presbyter for Mystagogy

In recent years, many have appealed to mystagogy as the solution to a variety of problems: mystagogy as the way to address the incomprehension of the liturgy by Christians and its seeming irrelevance to their spiritual life; mystagogy as the way to overcome ignorance of both liturgy and catechetics, thus providing a new catechetical synthesis; mystagogy as a means of bringing the liturgy to the center of the life of the church. In reality, at least for now, mystagogy remains more of a stated intention than a real practice. There is a simple reason for this: to do mystagogy, it is necessary to have mystagogues. Mystagogy is nothing more than a method. And so it will never become an ordinary practice of the church until the church's presbyters become mystagogues.

Since the council, one of the most important and meaningful achievements of our Christian communities is a deeper awareness and understanding of the Scriptures, obtained above all through the formation of small prayer and study groups and the rediscovery of *lectio divina*. At the same time, we must acknowledge today the difficulty our people have in articulating their liturgical knowledge. We must therefore ask, why has an understanding of the liturgy not developed in tandem with this deepening biblical knowledge? Why has the widespread passion for a deeper understanding of the mystery of God expressed in the Scriptures not been accompanied by a passion for the celebration of this mystery in the liturgy? Biblical knowledge is not authentic until it is reflected in a community celebration of God's covenant with his people. One among several possible responses to these questions is certainly the failure to interpret and study the liturgy from the Bible, in other words, an inability to understand the Bible as a decisive (though not exclusive) hermeneutical key to the liturgy.

Authentic mystagogy draws the connections between our liturgical rites and the biblical story, in the conviction that the Bible—both the Old Testament and the New—bears witness to the salvation event that is made present in the liturgy.[16] Therefore, the object of mystagogy is not the rite itself but the salvation event that is celebrated in the rite. The liturgy, just as much as the Scriptures, call for study and ever greater spiritual understanding. What a return to *lectio divina*, after centuries of neglect, has meant for the Christian community's relationship with the Scriptures is what a return to mystagogy, after centuries of neglect, will mean for its relationship with the liturgy.

It is this spiritual understanding of the liturgy that presbyters are called to develop each liturgical celebration. It is therefore urgent that the homily recover its natural mystagogical dimensions. The homilist must announce the salvation event both through the biblical readings and through the liturgical texts and gestures, demonstrating that the liturgy is the memorial of what the Scriptures narrate. The homilist must be able to wisely integrate biblical exegesis and liturgical exegesis. There can be no mystagogy without mystagogues, because only one who is initiated is able to initiate others; only one who has access to the mystery and has contemplated it can be a mystagogue. Only presbyters who are initiated into the mystery of God contained in the Scriptures and celebrated in the liturgy, presbyters for whom the word of God and the liturgy are the daily food of their spiritual lives are able to bring others to that mystery which they first have experienced. The mystagogical capacity is a true and proper gift of the Spirit. It is charism.

---

16. Cf. Nicola Albanesi, "La mistagogia: un modello di mistagogia sacramentaria," *Ephemerides Liturgicae* 112 (1998): 178–86.

# Chapter Seven

# The Missal, Book of the Prayer of the Church

*"The authority of the liturgy is superior to that of the fathers and of the theologians."*

—Prosper Gueranger[1]

## The Missal and the Scriptures

The description of the Missal as a book of prayer becomes all the more true when the primacy of the word of God contained in the Sacred Scriptures is fully understood.[2] (I use this word "contained," according to the expression of *Dei Verbum*: "The Sacred Scriptures contain the Word of God, and, because they are inspired, they are truly the Word

---

1. Prosper Gueranger, *Institutions liturgiques*, vol. 4, *Polémique liturgique*, 2nd ed. (Paris-Brussels: Société générale de librairie catholique, 1885), 370.

2. This chapter was originally published as "Il Messale è libro di preghiera," in *Celebrare il mistero di Cristo con il Messale. Atti del XLIII Convegno liturgico-pastorale dell' A.L.F. S. Cuore, Opera della Regalità di N.S.G.C.* (Milan: Centro Ambrosiano, 2002), 31–46.

of God."[3]) The primacy of the word of God contained in the Scriptures is a presupposition that is both theological and liturgical; indeed, we can say that it is properly theological because it is first of all liturgical. With respect to theology, the liturgy realizes the primacy of the word of God in a completely fundamental way, for in the liturgy the primacy of the word is *enacted* by the church. The eucharistic assembly (by definition the *ecclesia*) actualizes the primacy of the word of God when, celebrating its faith, it solemnly carries the Book of the Gospels in procession, incenses it, reads it, comments on it, kisses it; it does all of this because it believes that this book contains the word of God.

Therefore the Scriptures—and in a preeminent way the Book of the Gospels—are not only true and proper liturgical books; they are the liturgical book *par excellence* because of the essential role of the liturgy in the origins of the Christian Scriptures. The liturgical assembly, as the original place of the proclamation of the paschal faith, was the crucible, the milieu in which the Christian Scriptures developed. What, after all, is the New Testament, if not the original and, therefore, "canonical" witness of the church's paschal faith? It is in its assiduous attention to the Lord's Supper and to the breaking of the bread that the primitive church progressively gave form to the proclamation of its faith; and it is to this assiduousness that the evangelist Luke bears witness in the story of the disciples on the road to Emmaus: "When he was at table with them, he took bread, blessed and broke it, and gave it to them. Then their eyes were opened, and they recognized him" (Luke 24:30-31). "The ecclesial assembly," writes Pierre Grelot, "remains the place where the books are conserved, read, and explained, as it was the place where

---

3. Second Vatican Council, *Dei Verbum*, n. 24.

they were written."[4] Grelot notes that a fundamental criterion in the second and third centuries for discerning inspiration in the formation of the canon of Scripture was the proclamation of the various writings in the context of the church's liturgy.

But if the liturgy was the womb in which the Christian Scriptures were formed, it remains today their essential environment. When the texts of Sacred Scripture are proclaimed within a liturgical assembly, they come alive and fully become the word of God addressed "in act" to his people. In the Liturgy of the Word, God speaks. By speaking, God forms, molds, and creates the community. To recognize the primacy of the book of the Scriptures in the liturgy means above all to give obedience to the liturgy itself, which recognizes in the texts of Scripture a superior quality, normative beyond any other text with regard to the faith of the church.

The liturgy, then, establishes an *ordo* of the liturgical books, in which the Missal is neither the first nor the only one. But the Missal is certainly the book that interacts, more than any other, with the Scriptures. The liturgy itself establishes an essential relationship between the Missal and the Scriptures. The texts of the Missal are, in fact, nothing more than the response of the liturgical assembly to the proclamation of the Scriptures. This is so true that we can say that if there had been no hearing of the word of God contained in the Scriptures on the part of the church, we would have no Missal today. Without the hearing of the word of God in the church, there is no liturgical text, no Missal. The liturgical texts of the Missal are the mature fruit of the church's reception of the Scriptures.

4. Pierre Grelot and Christian Bigaré, *Introduction critique au Nouveau Testament*, vol. 5, *L'achèvement des Écritures* (Paris: DDB, 1977), 177.

They are purest essence of the church's reflection on the word of God. For this reason, we can say that the Missal is the result of the *lectio divina* that the church has carried out through the course of its history; *lectio, meditatio, oratio* are not only the stages of personal reading of the Scriptures that the Christian carries out in private but also the stages of development of every liturgy.

The Missal is the crystallization of the *lectio* of the church that has read the Scriptures attentively, meditated on them, and allowed that meditation to become spoken prayer.[5] Suffice it to recall here one of the most noted prefaces of the Roman liturgy, which is a true and proper *meditatio* on the story of Jesus' encounter with the Samaritan woman in John 4:

> For when he asked the Samaritan woman for water to drink,
> he had already created the gift of faith within her
> and so ardently did he thirst for her faith,
> that he kindled in her the fire of divine love.[6]

The meaning and value of this preface, like every liturgical text, is not simply to transmit certain content but to guide the reception of the Scriptures within the dynamic of the celebration of faith. The liturgy cannot be reduced to the simple ecclesial proclamation of the Scriptures, but such proclamation must be understood and lived as an integral aspect of the celebration of faith.

---

5. Cf. Enzo Bianchi, "La parola pregata: l'eucologia come risaltato dell'ascolto," in *Bibbia e liturgia*, II. *Scriptura crescit cum orante*, ed. A. N. Terrin (Padua: Messaggero-Abbazia di Santa Giustina, 1993), 49–67.

6. Preface for the Third Sunday of Lent, *The Roman Missal*, *Third Edition* (Collegeville, MN: Liturgical Press, 2011), 238.

This affirmation of the primacy of the word of God contained in the Scriptures and the essential relationship between the Missal and the Scriptures reminds us that the Missal always points beyond itself, always points to the Scriptures. This dynamic permeates the entire liturgical action. There is a true union between Scripture and Missal, a union that never lets us forget that the liturgy is the crucible and the womb of the Bible, and that the Missal is the mature fruit of the church's listening to the Scriptures. This union must be kept in mind in the study of the Scriptures, even in the most scholarly biblical exegesis; a liturgical exegesis and hermeneutic of the Scriptures has been too often neglected in the West, while in Orthodox biblical hermeneutics the liturgical tradition has been allowed to make a determinative contribution.[7] Every Christian—but in a particular way the pastor, the exegete, and the liturgist—must carry, so to speak, the Bible in one hand and the Missal in the other. Never the Bible without the Missal and never the Missal without the Bible.

## The Missal, Witness to the Link between *Lex Orandi* and *Lex Credendi*

Faithfully anchored to the foundation of the Scriptures, the Missal is a fundamental collection of texts in which the church expresses its faith and identifies itself. From the beginning, the church has always understood that the content of its prayer bore an essential connection with the content of its faith, that what it prayed expressed what it believed. In this sense, the Missal bears witness to the link between *lex orandi* and *lex credendi*. (The ancient adage is

---

7. Cf. John Breck, *The Power of the Word in the Worshiping Church* (Crestwood, NJ: St. Vladimir's Seminary Press, 1986).

*lex orandi, lex credendi*: "The law of prayer establishes the law of faith." It is attributed to the fifth-century monk, Prosper of Aquitaine.) The Missal is the normative and canonical *locus* of the prayer of the church that attests to the faith of the church. If the church has established a canon of the Scriptures, no less has it fixed the canon of its prayer through the ongoing creation and selection of liturgical texts. The church has understood that not all prayers can be liturgical prayers. In establishing the Missal, it is as though the church says to itself: here and nowhere else is contained your prayer. It says to every Christian: here and nowhere else is the canon of your prayer.

The Missal, understood as the *ordo orationis*—that is, as the norm of the words (texts) and gestures (rite) of the church's prayer—is therefore a preeminent witness of the relationship between *lex orandi* and *lex credendi*. To truly understand Prosper's adage means to recognize that the *lex orandi*—understood in its vastness and complexity— provides access in an immediate and complete way to the church's faith. Paul De Clerck has observed that "the *lex orandi*, understood as the universal prayer of the church set on its scriptural foundation, points the way of the *lex credendi*, the correct way of believing."[8]

The "Amen," through which the assembly affirms and ratifies the content of the liturgical text, is in fact the highest expression of the church's awareness that its faith is expressed in every liturgical prayer. For this reason, there is no liturgical prayer without the assembly's Amen, without that seal through which the assembly says: "Yes, this is our prayer, this is the prayer of the church." The liturgical Amen is, so to speak, a corollary of the confession of the article of faith, "I believe in the church"; that "I believe in the church"

---

8. Paul De Clerck, *"Lex orandi, lex credendi*. Un principe heuristique," *La Maison-Dieu* 222 (2000): 71.

implicitly contains an "I believe what the church prays."
The liturgical Amen makes explicit what is implicit in the
creed; it is the assent of faith to the church's prayer. Through
the Amen, the assembly declares its faith in what it prays.

The Missal, a witness of the relationship between *lex
orandi* and *lex credendi*, therefore points the sure way toward
the correct manner of belief. But are we convinced today,
both in theological reflection on the church's faith and in
the lived experience of the church, that the liturgy truly indicates the right manner of believing? Are we convinced that
the words and the gestures of the prayer contained in the
Missal can be the authoritative place for knowing and learning the faith of the church? Are we convinced that teaching
someone to pray is also teaching them to believe, and that
in learning to pray one learns to believe? Are we aware today
of the role that the liturgy plays in the understanding that
Christians have about their faith? Do we possess that level
of understanding shown by the early leaders of the liturgical
movement, such as Prosper Gueranger when he wrote in
his *Institutions liturgiques*, "The authority of the liturgy is
superior to that of the fathers and the theologians"?[9] Paraphrasing Gueranger, we can say that with regard to the faith,
the Christian learns more from the liturgy than from the
fathers of the church or from theologians.

## The Missal, Matrix of Prayer

Let us consider one aspect of this matter a bit more
carefully. If the Scriptures and the tradition are the *regula
fidei*, the Missal is certainly the *regula orationis*: the model,
the criterion, the norm of Christian prayer. It is as though,
through the Missal, the church says to every Christian:
"Take, read: this is the canon of your prayer."

9. Prosper Guéranger, *Institutions liturgiques*, 4:370.

The Missal is the matrix of Christian prayer in the sense that it presents the image of Christian prayer like a die bears the imprint of an image so that it can then be used to reproduce the image on another surface. The Missal preserves the fundamental imprint of Christian prayer; with this primary image as a basis, authentic prayer is reproduced in the life of every believer. The Missal teaches the grammar of Christian prayer: what it is, to whom it is addressed, how it is formulated, what it asks.

Among the many liturgical texts found in the Missal, the eucharistic prayer is not only the euchological text of greatest importance; it is also the highest and most expressive synthesis of Christian prayer. In its content, structure, and dynamic, the anaphora represents the microcosm of Christian prayer. The believer who allows it to penetrate her spiritual understanding has certainly begun to approach the heart of Christian prayer.

Above all, the anaphora teaches the Christian the movement of prayer and to whom prayer is addressed. The eucharistic prayer is always addressed to the Father, through the Son, in the Holy Spirit. This is the dynamic of the eucharistic prayer because it is the dynamic of the revelation of the mystery of God. Revelation is the revelation of the Father, through the Son, in the power of the Holy Spirit; the movement of revelation forms the movement of the act of faith, of which prayer is an essential part. With rare exceptions, the ancient anaphoric tradition attests that prayer is addressed always to God the Father, putting it in perfect continuity with Jewish prayer and at the same time obeying *sine glossa* the command of Jesus to his disciples: "When you pray say, 'Father'" (cf. Luke 11:2; Matt 6:9). The anaphora is addressed to the Father because it is the prayer of the church, which is the body of Christ; it is prayer in the Son. By addressing the Father in one's prayer, the Christian is always aware that her prayer, even in private, is never the prayer of one person, an individual, but it is the prayer of that community of sons and daughters, brothers and sisters, of which she is a part. The prayer addressed to the Father witnesses to the radical impossibility of Christian prayer of being private, because when a Christian prays, the entire church prays in her.

The anaphora, then, teaches Christians the nature of their prayer: it is the action of grace in the double movement of anamnesis and intercession. In the anamnesis one makes memorial of the *mirabilia Dei*, the works of salvation accomplished by God in human history. The prayer of the Christian must therefore be, above all, a memorial of God's action, because it is only from what God has done for humanity that humanity knows who God is. Starting from the anamnesis one is inserted into the movement of intercession, where one asks God to continue today and in the future that which he has accomplished in the past.

The anaphora teaches the Christian what to ask for. Suffice it to recall here the three gifts that the eucharistic prayers of the liturgical tradition constantly ask of God on behalf of the church: unity, peace, and perfection in love. Paul refers to these elements in his letter to the Christians of Ephesus, exhorting them to bear with one another in love, seeking to preserve the unity of the Spirit in the bond of peace (cf. Eph 4:2-3). The intercession of the anaphora confirms that the spirit of the liturgy is identical to the spirit of the apostolic church, witnessed to by the Scriptures and by which the liturgy was formed. It is a spirit that we find, for example, in Ignatius of Antioch, when he invites the Christians of Philadelphia to seek unity in the Eucharist: "Be eager, then, to celebrate one Eucharist; for one is the flesh of our Lord Jesus Christ, and one the cup for union through his blood: one the altar, just as one the bishop along with the presbytery and deacons."[10] The church is truly the body of Christ when it is one, when it lives that full communion that is the fruit of love and of peace. For this reason, liturgical prayer is limited to asking for unity, peace, and charity, demonstrating a wise awareness of what the church is and exactly what makes it the church. Liturgical prayer teaches Christians that not just anything ought to be the object of their petitions to God but only that which is essential and vital.

I wish to mention briefly one element of the anaphora too often absent and ignored in the prayer of the individual Christian. The anaphora demonstrates that Christian prayer must be *cosmic* prayer, offered in communion with all of creation. Eucharistic Prayer IV reminds us that we pray "giving voice to every creature under heaven."[11] In this the prayer calls to mind the psalter, which concludes Psalm 150 by singing, "Let everything that breathes praise the LORD!" (Ps 150:6). Within the human voice that sings the glory of the thrice-holy God, we hear the voice of every created being, those thinking and unthinking, animate and inanimate. Among God's creation, only the human person can take all of creation in her hands to offer it in thanksgiving to God, thus becoming the priest of creation. In its "giving voice to every creature under heaven," the anaphora bears witness that every Christian must widen his prayer to include all creation, for in the one who prays, all creation groans, expressing its eager longing for the revelation of the children of God (see Rom 8:19).

10. Ignatius of Antioch, "Letter to the Philadelphians," in *Ignatius of Antioch: A Commentary on the Letters of Ignatius of Antioch*, trans. William R. Schoedel, Hermeneia (Philadelphia: Fortress Press, 1985), 197.

11. Preface of Eucharistic Prayer IV, *The Roman Missal*, 656.

A final element to which I wish to turn in this brief consideration of liturgical prayer as matrix of Christian prayer is one that is proper and perhaps exclusive to the texts of the *Roman Missal*. More than any other Euchology, that of the *Roman Missal* teaches the Christian the simplicity and the essentiality of prayer. Compared to the texts of other Christian liturgical traditions, both Eastern and Western, the texts of the Roman liturgy are characterized by their *concinnitas*, that is, for their sober elegance, brevity, and concision. These characteristics represent the "genius" of the Roman liturgy. To compare, for example, the fullness and the prolixity of a Mozarabic *illatio* with the concise style of the Latin preface, the difference is surprising. The essentiality of Roman liturgical texts seems to be a reflection of the liturgical architectural style within which they were born: the Romanesque and the gothic, severe architectonic styles in its lines and essential in its forms.

The pedagogy of Latin liturgical prayer guides Christians through a slow and difficult journey of weeding out from her personal prayer all but what is essential, an elimination of whatever is superfluous, a purification of content and form. Romano Guardini wrote, "Liturgical prayer must be a long and severe discipline,"[12] and I believe the concept of discipline befits very well the characteristics of the pedagogy of the Roman liturgy.

This liturgy offers a true spiritual discipline that is in profound harmony with the ancient teaching of the fathers of the church on prayer. They insisted on the importance of not distracting oneself with many words and long formulas. In the twenty-eighth chapter of the *Scala Paradisi*, St. John Climacus admonishes, "Talkative prayer

---

12. Romano Guardini, *Formazione Liturgica. Saggi* (Milan: OR, 1988), 91.

frequently distracts the mind and deludes it, whereas brevity makes for concentration."[13] A single word, the essence, keeps the one who prays from becoming distracted or fragmented. Commenting on the prayer of the fathers of Egyptian monasticism, John Cassian noted, "They delight more in understanding the text than in sheer volume."[14] And finally the sentence of a father of the desert, Antioch of San Saba (the Monk), who describes a monk's prayer by means of a paradox: "The prayer of the monk must be incessant and brief."[15]

The liturgical texts of the *Roman Missal* testify, then, in their own way, to the simplicity, the essentiality, and the brevity that mark Christian prayer. My prayer that must be at the same time incessant and brief: it is incessant when my entire existence becomes a sacrifice of praise, and it is brief when, after long discipline, it has arrived at what is essential, nothing more and nothing less than what is needed.

## The Task of the Missal Today

One of the cardinal tasks of the liturgical movement was to make the liturgy known and understood by Christians. In achieving the goal, the so-called missal of the faithful played a fundamental role. Lefebvre in the French-speaking countries and Caronti in Italy, not to mention others, encouraged the people to follow the liturgy through translations of texts read by those who presided over the celebration.

13. John Climacus, *The Ladder of Divine Ascent*, trans. Colm Luibheid and Norman Russell (New York: Paulist Press, 1982), 275.

14. John Cassian, *The Monastic Institutes*, trans. Jerome Bertram (London: Saint Austin Press, 1999), 22.

15. Antioco di San Saba, *Pandette* 26, PG 89:1516.

This acknowledged the importance of the faithful knowing what was happening in the liturgy. The "missals of the faithful" were, in other words, an expression of an awareness on the part of the pioneers of the liturgical movement that only to the extent that Christians could take in their hands the texts of the Missal, read them, understand them, and meditate on them, would it be possible for them to appropriate the faith celebrated by the liturgy and, by understanding the content, to participate in the liturgical action by fully living the mystery that is celebrated.

To describe the task of the Missal today means first of all to understand the role that it plays in the believers' knowledge of the liturgical texts. It means, in other words, to accept the primacy of interiorization or personal appropriation by Christians of all that is said and done in the liturgy. In recent decades, we have insisted perhaps too much on an exteriorization of the liturgy that emphasizes the need to express one's feelings and emotions, with the aim of a climate marked by encounter and celebration. Today we are rediscovering that the liturgy, more than being the gathering together of the emotions of a particular group of people, is above all the "interiorization," or acceptance of a Word that has called the assembly together and nourished the assembly that it might live what it has received. The liturgical celebration must always be for the Christian the moment of interiorization. We must experience the liturgy as hearing the Word, as prayer, as real encounter with God. In a lucid passage on the future of the liturgy, the theologian Louis-Marie Chauvet wrote:

> In the future, the liturgy will probably have to honor, more than it has in the past, the need for a more prayerful atmosphere, expressed today by a rather generalized cultural tendency. It will probably also need to be particularly vigilant to ensure that the current desire for

"spirituality," which we see expressed in many ways, does not lead little by little to a liturgy that is overly personal in style. In any case, in a world that is no longer Christian in character, the faithful seem to experience more and more the need to find in the liturgy a place where they can establish or reestablish themselves as "subjects" of the Christian faith.[16]

In order truly to be the book of the church's prayer, the Missal must once again become the book of the prayer of the individual Christians and, in a particular way, the book of the prayer of the shepherd whose role is to preside over the prayer of the Christian community and to teach the community to pray. This means we must review carefully the texts of liturgical prayer, to read them, meditate on them, penetrate them in order to interiorize them deeply. One who enters deeply into the liturgical texts will remain there and grow as a person and as a Christian. Romano Guardini for good reason wrote, "The 'exterior' person can easily experience liturgical prayer as untrue, because the voice that speaks in the liturgy is profound, authentic."[17] In the liturgy, one is formed and built up as a Christian.

Acknowledging the need for Christians to know the texts of the Missal does not mean somehow to reduce the liturgy purely to an object of study. It does not mean to perform a purely noetic and intellectual exercise. When the texts of the liturgy are assimilated and understood in depth, they become a source of understanding of the mystery that they celebrate. Understanding the liturgical text in fact uniquely impacts one's relationship with God.

16. Louis-Marie Chauvet, "La liturgie demain: essai de perspective," in *La liturgie, lieu théologique*, ed. P. De Clerck (Paris: Beauchesne, 1999), 213.

17. Guardini, *Formazione liturgica*, 91.

As it was at the dawn of the liturgical movement, the Missal remains today a privileged and decisive tool for addressing the current disconnect between liturgy and ecclesial life. The Missal as a book of prayer remains an essential means for reestablishing an authentic relationship, seen clearly in recent generations, between what one prays, what one knows, and the way one lives. An authentic relationship between what the liturgy transmits and what Christians live is essential for a living faith today. Christian life constantly faces the risk of drifting into an individualism of faith, which suggests that faith is simply a matter of one's personal beliefs. The liturgy, as communal celebration of the act of faith, discourages every form of subjectivism and personalism of faith. Without an assiduous attentiveness to the communal celebration of the act of faith, faith is reduced to gnosis that hopelessly consigns the Christian to a spiritual ideology of intellectual convictions and meanings that have little to do with the faith of the church. The liturgy, then, is no longer a celebration of the faith of the church but a cultivation of an individual's spiritual instincts.

# Chapter Eight

# The Liturgy, School of Prayer

*"Yes, you can pray at home, but not in the same way as you can in the church."*

—John Chrysostom[1]

## Christian Liturgy and Prayer

To understand the liturgy as a school of prayer is essential, not only for extrinsic reasons but because of the very nature of Christian worship.[2] The worship of Christians is essentially different from both the Jewish and pagan sacrificial economies that preceded it, because the sacrifice it calls for is not ritual but existential. It is realized in the offering of oneself, of one's entire life. For this reason

---

1. John Chrysostom, *On the Incomprehensible Nature of God*, trans. Paul W. Harkins, The Fathers of the Church 72 (Washington, DC: Catholic University of America Press, 1982), 110.

2. This chapter was originally published as "La formazione alla preghiera" in *La formazione liturgica*, ed. Andrea Grillo (Rome: CLV-Edizione liturgiche, 2006), 168–82; republished as *La liturgia, scuola di preghiera*, Testi di meditazione 143 (Bose: Qiqajon, 2006).

the church has always recognized in Paul's admonition in the Letter to the Romans—"present your bodies as a living sacrifice, holy and acceptable to God, which is your spiritual worship [*loghikè latreía*]" (Rom 12:1)—as a full expression of the truth about worship.

The Pauline expression *loghikè latreía* includes a plurality of meanings that are profoundly coherent and complementary to each other. While the Bible of the Italian Episcopal Conference chooses to translate the phrase as "culto spirituale,"[3] the expression can be understood most literally as "worship according to the *lógos*" or "conforming oneself to the *lógos*," referring to the *Lógos* incarnate who is Jesus Christ, giving the expression a strongly Christological connotation. But *loghikè latreía* can also be translated as "worship according to reason,"[4] "rational worship," or simply "logical worship," as we see in more recent French translations of the Bible: "C'est là le culte logique que vous lui devez."[5] These possibilities are expressed in the *Traduction œcuménique de la Bible*, which, translating the phrase as "culte spirituel," observes in a footnote: "Spiritual or logical or reasonable. The adjective used here often serves, especially in Hebrew or Greek authors, to designate true worship, which involves the whole person, as opposed to a merely exterior and formal worship."[6] In addition to these other translations, one might also render *loghikè latreía* as "worship by word" or "worship carried out through words"; this final approach is particularly important for our reflections here, because it makes clear that

3. ["Spiritual worship"—Trans.]

4. As it is rendered in *La sacra Bibbia* (Rome: Edizione Paoline, 1968), 1202.

5. *La Bible* (Paris: Bayard, 2001), 2494.

6. *Traduction œcuménique de la Bible* (Paris: Alliance Biblique Universelle-Cerf, 1994), 1647, n. f.

the ritual manifestation of existential worship happens through a worship by word, that is, through prayer.

It is *lógos*, the word, that distinguishes the human person in a determinant way from every other living being. The word is the particular and highest expression of the human body and of the totality of the human person. The word, we might say, is the truth about the person and, in the word, humanity finds and expresses its truth. To be word is to be relationship, and the more fully word we are, the more fully are we ourselves. Prayer, which is the human word to God, represents the authentic sacrifice. It is in prayer—that is, through being in relationship with God—that the human person reaches her fullness and becomes *lógos*, and this is the sacrifice offered to God. Prayer becomes sacrifice when the words of praise, thanksgiving, and blessing that are spoken express and contain in truth the person's offering of her whole life to God. When a Christian expresses in liturgy the truth of her existential worship, she offers no other sacrifice to God than the sacrifice of prayer, the sacrifice of praise. In other words, the prayer of thanksgiving is the sacrifice offered to God—above all in the Eucharist, but not only there. As the ancient anaphoric tradition attests, the Eucharist is a sacrifice of word, because the giving of thanks is nothing other than prayer.[7] Yes, to give thanks is to offer sacrifice.

So the Pauline concept of *loghikè latreía* reveals the truth of Christian worship, an existential worship that is, when expressed in its ritual form, worship by word. If the liturgy were not *loghikè latreía*, it would not be prayer, would not be authentic Christian worship. For this reason, to reflect

---

7. Cf. Enrico Mazza, "L'eucharistia come sacrificio nella testimonianza della tradizione anaforica," in *L'idea di sacrificio. Un approccio di teologia liturgica*, ed. E. Mazza (Bologna: EDB, 2002), 117–54.

on the liturgy as the school of prayer is not optional but essential. The liturgy is the decisive (though not exclusive) place in which the Christian learns to pray.

The relationship between liturgy and prayer is therefore clear enough that I need not demonstrate it further. I wish, rather, to offer my reflections on the liturgy as a school of prayer in two parts. First, I will consider the *subject* of the formation, the person who learns to pray. Second, I will consider the *way* the liturgy teaches us to pray, focusing on three elements of liturgical prayer: hearing, interiorization, and interpretation.

## Through the Liturgy, God Teaches His People to Pray

That the liturgy is the decisive place for the formation of Christians in prayer is certainly clear, and one would find wide agreement with the idea throughout the church. But we must be clear that it is God who is at work in the liturgy, teaching us to pray, for the liturgy is above all and primarily the work of God. *Sacrosanctum Concilium* defines the liturgy as *opus Christi*,[8] and if the liturgical constitution, as is sometimes observed, failed to take sufficient account of the Holy Spirit's role in the liturgy,[9] this lacuna is amply remedied by the *Catechism of the Catholic Church*, a text that in many ways represents a point of no return in Western doctrine on the topic. There we read: "In the liturgy the Holy Spirit is teacher of the faith of the People of God and artisan of 'God's masterpieces,' the sacraments of the

---

8. Cf. Second Vatican Council, *Sacrosanctum Concilium*, n. 7.

9. The topic is addressed instead in *Lumen Gentium*, which affirms that in the liturgy "through the sacramental signs, the power of the Holy Spirit acts on us" (n. 50).

New Covenant."[10] To say, then, that the liturgy teaches Christians to pray does mean that the church acts pedagogically there, like a mother teaching her children to pray. But God is the first teacher of prayer in the liturgy. Certainly, God's action and the church's action in the liturgy are not opposed to one another but neither can they be indistinctly confused. They must be distinguished, articulated, and above all ordered correctly. Even if the church is the integral subject of the liturgical action, it remains always the receiver and not the actor of the *opus salutis* that happens there. In the same way, the church is always the receiver of the liturgy's education in prayer. The well-known sentence of Cyprian—"You cannot have God for your Father if you have not the Church for your mother"[11]— must be adapted to say that one who is not aware of having God as father in learning to pray cannot have the church's liturgy as mother in this task.

The Bible attests to this in the way it describes God's work on behalf of Israel and the nature of God's relationship with his people. Indeed, the very term "Father" to designate God has a clear educative connotation: "From heaven he made you hear his voice to discipline you," said Moses to the people in Deuteronomy 4:36. Certainly the Deuteronomist, more than any other biblical author, interprets the exodus as a work of education carried out by God on behalf of the people of Israel.[12] The apex of this understanding appears in Deuteronomy 8:3-5:

10. *Catechism of the Catholic Church,* n. 1091.

11. Cyprian of Carthage, *The Unity of the Catholic Church,* trans. Maurice Bévenot, Ancient Christian Writers 25 (Westminster, MD: Newman Press, 1957), 48–49.

12. That the exodus was the great educative work of God is seen also in the Greek word *éxodus,* which literally means "departing journey," and in the Latin verb *educere,* from which is derived the

[The LORD] humbled you by letting you hunger, then by feeding you with manna, with which neither you nor your ancestors were acquainted, in order to make you understand that one does not live by bread alone, but by every word that comes from the mouth of the LORD. . . . Know then in your heart that as a parent disciplines a child so the LORD your God disciplines you.

The Lord teaches Israel like a father teaches his son, and the forty years in the desert represent the time of Israel's education. The *paideía* of God has as its purpose the life, the happiness, and above all the freedom of the people whom he has released from slavery.

In the book of Exodus, we see that in this work of education for freedom, worship is both the purpose and the instrument. Worship is above all the purpose of the exodus, according to the command that the Lord repeats six times to Pharaoh through Moses: "Let my people go, so that they may worship me in the wilderness" (Exod 7:16; 7:26; 8:16; 9:1; 9:13; 10:3). Here worship—'*avodà*—refers in particular to sacrificial offering. But worship is not only the purpose of the exodus but also the instrument by which God forms Israel for freedom. The journey in the desert is the time during which God teaches the people how to adore him, revealing that learning to offer true worship to God means also learning to be a free people. If real freedom presupposes adoration of the one, true God, it is also the case that true worship demands a free people.

The biblical authors attest that worship is a fundamental instrument of God's *paideía* by attributing the liturgical order directly to God. In minute detail, God lays out the ways, the instruments, the times, and the places of Israel's

---

Italian *educare* [and the English *to educate*—Trans.], which literally means "to bring outside of."

worship. The people worship according to the Lord's precise commands. By presenting God as the architect and originator of Israel's worship, the biblical authors affirm a fundamental truth of its confession of faith: it is God who acts in worship, the Lord who is the primary actor in Israel's liturgy. This is the reason that the detailed liturgical prescriptions—found above all in Numbers and Leviticus but also in Exodus and Deuteronomy—are an integral part of the Torah. They affirm that the liturgical norms are part of the fundamental nucleus of Israel's faith, the Lord's own teaching. Indeed, the most correct translation of the term *Torà* is not "law" but "teaching," confirming the recognition of Scripture and the rabbinical tradition of the Torah's educative function. In sum, only through obeying the Torah's commands of justice, morality, and worship could Israel truly be a free people.

Scripture, then, bears witness that worship is the place where God acts, educating his people for service, for adoration, and so for prayer. This biblical truth also pervades the Christian liturgy; there, too, God is the primary actor, and the liturgy is above all God's action, God's work. Perhaps this biblical truth needs some reaffirmation today, after decades of well-established and almost exclusive use in Catholic theology of the Greek term *leitourghía* to designate the prayer of the church. We have largely forgotten the ancient term *opus Dei*, used—as the still-valid study of Irénée Hausherr shows—by the first Christian authors, and, in continuity with them, Benedict in his Rule, to refer to the church's prayer.[13] The etymology of *leitourghía* (*érgon toû laoû*) emphasizes the action of the church, making it the subject of liturgical action. But one can never

---

13. Cf. Irénée Hausherr, *Études de spiritualite orientale* (Rome: Pontificum institute orientalium studiorum, 1969), 121–44.

forget that there is no authentic *leitourghía* that is not at the same time *theourghía* (*érgon toû Theoû*), the action of God, *opus Dei*. The Eastern liturgical tradition has maintained its awareness of this biblical truth, speaking of the eucharistic synaxis as "Divine Liturgy." Here the adjective "divine" stands as a compliment of specification, insisting that the Divine Liturgy is that liturgy in which God acts. Catholic liturgical studies today must adjust its vocabulary in order to reaffirm the eminently theological nature of Christian liturgy.

The necessary first step to understanding the liturgy as the school of prayer, then, is to be aware that the Father, through the Son and in the Holy Spirit, is the one who teaches believers to pray in the liturgy. This leads us to consider the constitutive elements of the dynamic of Christian prayer that we learn from liturgy.

## Hearing, Interiorization, and Interpretation

Liturgical prayer follows a movement, a dynamic composed of three elements that follow one upon the other: hearing the word of God contained in the Scriptures, interiorization of the word that is heard, and finally, interpretation. The liturgy, by inserting the believer into this movement of prayer, teaches the believer a true and proper *ordo orationis*. To analyze this *ordo orationis*, I will take as a reference point the Divine Office or Liturgy of the Hours. In particular, we will consider the praying of the psalms.

### The Primacy of Hearing the Word of God

The liturgy teaches believers to pray first of all by teaching the primacy of hearing the word of God contained in the Scriptures. In Judeo-Christian revelation, hearing is the essential and constitutive dimension of prayer. Affirming this means relativizing the human word, making it secondary; it is a response. In Scripture, God is not defined in terms of essence, and the experience of God is not primarily experience of vision. Rather, God is defined in terms of relation, dialogue, word, and so the only possible experience of God is through hearing. The prophet Jeremiah said, "[T]his command I gave them, 'Obey my voice, and I will be your God, and you shall be my people'" (Jer 7:23). Roland Barthes, reflecting on the phenomenology of hearing, rightly observes that "the injunction of hearing is the total appeal of one subject to another . . . for which 'listen to me' means 'touch me, know that I exist.'"[14] And so when God enjoins *"Shema' Jisra'el"* (Deut 6:4), he is calling the people to confess his existence, to discern his presence. It is an invitation to enter into relation with an Other who precedes them and supports them. The strong awareness we find in the Jewish faith of the primacy of hearing in one's relationship with God is fully manifested in the fact that Israel's prayer *par excellence* is the *Shema'*. It is the repetition of the command to listen addressed to them by God. While other peoples might address prayers to other gods with the invocation, "Hear, O god!" the people of the covenant pray, "Hear, O Israel!" subverting the human phenomenon of prayer.

There is an important element at the beginning of the Divine Office, by which the liturgy teaches believers about the condition of possibility of every prayer. The Divine Office begins with the invocation, *"Domine, labia mea aperies. Et os meum annuntiabit laudem tuam"* (Lord, open my lips, and my mouth will proclaim your praise.) This verse of Psalm 50 (51), placed by the church as the first act and the first word of the one who prays, is more than simply a helpful opening line for prayer; it is the principle guide

---

14. Roland Barthes, Roland Havas, s.v., "Ascolto," in *Enciclopedia I*, ed. R. Romano (Torino: Einaudi, 1977), 985.

of the prayer. The invocation "Lord, open my lips" is the very definition of Christian prayer, insofar as it expresses an awareness that God is the origin of all prayer. We ask God to open our lips, recognizing that he is not only the origin of our praise but also the cause and the reason for it. God—that is, his word and his action carried out in history—is the condition of possibility of the prayer of the believer. Said another way, I can pray to God only because God first made himself known to humanity. To affirm the primacy of the word of God in prayer means therefore to affirm the primacy of the revelation of God, a primacy that extends even to my prayer.

The liturgy, then, in having believers pray Psalm 50 (51), teaches us that God is the condition of the possibility of our prayer and that the prayer we begin is above all God's work: it is God who opens our lips. The Byzantine office attests to this truth even further, with the initial invocation, "Lord, who have made me to get up from my bed and from sleep, illuminate my intelligence and my heart, open my lips so that I may sing to you, O holy Trinity." The liturgy of the East and the West are in agreement, then, in attributing to God the origin and the possibility of every prayer. This same understanding is found too in one of the most well-known passages on prayer, that of Evagrius Ponticus: "If you want to pray, you have need of God 'who bestows prayer on the one who prays' (1 Kgs 2:9)."[15]

Just as André Chouraqui was able to write, in his introduction to the psalter, "We [Jews] are born with this book

---

15. Evagrius of Pontus, "Chapters on Prayer," in *Evagrius of Pontus: The Greek Ascetic Corpus*, trans. Robert E. Sinkewicz (Oxford, UK: Oxford University Press, 2003), 199.

in our viscera,"[16] we can also say that Christian liturgy is born also with the psalter in its womb. But the Christian liturgy is not only born with the psalter in its womb; it has generated Christians through the praying of the psalms. The psalms, which are both the word of God and human prayer, bear witness that hearing of the word of God contained in the Scriptures is the matrix of Christian prayer. The ancient church understood the praying of the psalms as Christian prayer *par excellence*, and certainly all liturgical prayer must be strongly marked by the primacy of the word of God contained in the Scriptures. Passages of Scripture are woven throughout the ancient anaphoric texts, to the point that the German liturgist Achim Budde, in his recent study of the Alexandrian version of the anaphora of Basil, writes of a true and proper "biblicism" of this text.[17]

For this reason, all that is said and done within the liturgy must have a biblical basis; the liturgical words and gestures must have the Scriptures as their norm. Inasmuch as the Scriptures are the native language of the liturgy, hearing is at the roots of liturgical prayer. If the liturgy speaks the language of the Scriptures, then over time liturgical prayer nourishes the believer in the Word. It creates in us a *mens biblica*, a biblical heart, and a prayer life marked by the primacy of the Word.

A saying attributed to Abba Pambo demonstrates the anxiety already felt by some in the fourth century over the displacement of the primacy of the word of God from Christian liturgy. Starting from the fourth century in Egypt, the monastic liturgy, until then characterized uniquely by

---

16. André Chouraqui, *Il Cantico dei cantici e introduzione ai Salmi* (Rome: Citta Nuova, 1980), 153.

17. Cf. Achim Budde, *Die* ägyptische *Basilios-Anaphora* (Münster: Aschendorff, 2004).

prayer of the psalms and other texts of Scripture, began to be influenced by other compositions with origins in episcopal liturgies. Expressing his opposition to these poetic innovations in the liturgy, Abba Pambo harshly reproached one of his disciples who had learned some tropes from the cathedral liturgy of Alexandria, saying to him:

> Woe to us, my son! We are close to the times when monks will abandon solid food, the word of the Holy Spirit, in favor of hymns and melodies. . . . I tell you, my son, that there will come a time when Christians will discard the books of the holy apostles and the prophets of God, when they will scrape away the words from the scrolls of the holy Scriptures in order to write tropes and speeches in the Hellenizing styles.[18]

Abba Pambo's prophecy seems to be effectively realized in the Eastern liturgy, where ecclesiastical compositions have progressively taken the upper hand over the texts of Scripture. The Western liturgical sources testify that in the West, from the sixth to the twelfth centuries, the monastic liturgy was essentially psalmic prayer; but with the Middle Ages, when monks were ordained presbyters and the number of Masses celebrated multiplied, psalmody diminished progressively. One passage, probably Cistercian, conserved in a manuscript of the thirteenth century, attests to the regret of one witness to this evolution:

> It is significant that where today masses are celebrated, the ancients sung the psalms. But the young are no longer in favor of long prayers and the difficult (*laboriosa*) sing-

---

18. Detti dei padre, Serie anomina J 758, in *I padri del deserto, Detti editi e inediti*, ed. Sabino Chiala and Lisa Cremaschi (Bose: Qiqajon, 2002), 168. [My translation from the Italian.—Trans.]

ing of the psalmody. They prefer a great number of masses (*missarum moltitudinem*) celebrated quickly (*citissimam*), but that is extremely dangerous and to be feared. The difference, in fact, between applying oneself to masses and to the many psalms is that the one who eats unworthily from the table of the Lord eats and drinks his own condemnation, while the sinner who, in the presence of the angels, sings the psalms with the attention of spirit and mind, not only does not incur condemnation, but even obtains the pardon of sins.[19]

The primacy of the word of God in the liturgy represents a unique aspect of Christian prayer.

## The Interiorization of Prayer

Communal prayer rooted in hearing the word of God must be personally interiorized by every person who prays. This process of personal interiorization of communal prayer is of great importance in the formation in prayer that is accomplished by the liturgy. If the liturgy does not teach this interiorization, it does not accomplish its educative purpose. It is essential that the liturgy predispose each person who gathers to appropriate in himself what he hears proclaimed. It must offer periods of listening and periods of silence, so that the one who prays may be nourished by the spiritual meaning of the liturgical text. This interiorization is the purpose of listening, insofar as "listening is a game of catch played with meanings."[20]

Monastic teaching insists often on the necessity of singing the psalms with understanding as a condition of authentic prayer. Suffice it here to evoke the admonition of

19. Cited in Jacques Leclercq, "Anciennes sentences monastiques," *Collectanea cisterciensia* 14 (1952): 120n8.
20. Barthes and Havas, s.v., "Ascolto," 988.

Basil of Caesarea, which compares the praying of a psalm with eating a meal:

> Q[UESTION]: What is it to "sing psalms wisely"? (Ps 46:7 LXX)
> R[ESPONSE]: Just as with all foods, the flavour of each is discerned through taste, so also are prudence and discernment with the words of Holy Scripture. "For the throat," it says, "tastes foods, but the sense discerns words" (cf. Job 12:11; 34:3 LXX). Therefore if one's soul is intent on each word of the psalms, as taste is intent on distinguishing the flavour of foods, such a one fulfils that which is said: "sing psalms wisely" (Ps 46:7).[21]

John Cassian, who lived his monastic life in the monasteries of southern Egypt, offers in his *Institutions* and *Conferences* detailed descriptions of the way Egyptian monks prayed the psalms. He writes: "All the others sat . . . and directed their attention [*intentio cordis*, perhaps the biblical *kawwanat ha-lev*] to the words of the psalmist. He sang eleven psalms, on an even tone, with no pause between verses but separated by collects. The twelfth psalm he sang with an Alleluia response."[22] According to this description, the praying of psalms proceeds along a precise pattern, articulated in two parts. The first part is the hearing of the psalm sung alone by one monk. All are seated; it is a bodily posture of listening. The second part of this unique dynamic of psalmody is that which Cassian calls *interiectio orationis*—a pause, a parenthesis of silent prayer between one

21. Basil of Caesarea, *The Rule of St Basil in Latin and English: A Revised Critical Edition*, Question 110, trans. Anna M. Silvas (Collegeville, MN: Liturgical Press, 2013), 197.

22. John Cassian, *The Monastic Institutes* 2.5, trans. Jerome Bertram (London: Saint Austin Press, 1999), 19.

psalm and the next. What Cassian describes is a true *ordo orationis psalmorum*, characterized by a precise rhythm, a sort of systolic and diastolic of prayer. Such a rhythm affirms both the primacy of hearing the word of God contained in the psalms and the necessity of a silent, interior prayer after each psalm that allows spiritual understanding to develop. Later in the *Institutions*, Cassian justifies the reduced number of psalms—no longer twelve for each office—and the times of silence between them by saying, "They delight more in understanding the text than in sheer volume. They follow the phrase, 'I will sing in the spirit, but I will also sing in my mind' (1 Cor 14:15) with all their might."[23]

"*Psallam et mente*," is the way Jerome translated Paul's expression in 1 Corinthians, suggesting that the interiorization of liturgical prayer, its personal appropriation, is an operation of spiritual understanding and discernment. The liturgical text first comes from outside of the one who hears it, but true hearing makes the text an interior reality as well, producing echoes and resonances within. This is the meaning of Isaac of Nineveh's admonition:

> In the verses of your song and your prayer, pay attention not to be one who passes on words coming from a stranger. . . . Pronounce those words as though they are your own, pleading, with discernment . . . as one who is aware of the true meaning of what he does.[24]

Interiorization is truly accomplished only by one who "is aware of the true meaning of what he does." It is

23. Ibid., 2.11, p. 22.
24. Isaac of Nineveh, *Prima collezione* 53. [My translation from the Italian.—Trans.]

*cum-prehendere*, a taking within oneself and into oneself. It is appropriation of the spiritual meaning of the text.

The dynamic of interiorization must therefore be at the heart of the liturgy. When the texts and gestures are not interiorized by those who participate in liturgy, they cannot nourish the Christian and form her identity. In many ways today, we see a real and strong (but only vaguely articulated) need for interiority, for a more interior relationship with the divine, expressed by our contemporaries. This is true within the church, where believers desire to experience a more deeply interior prayer, but they rarely find it in the context of typical liturgies.

All of this calls for careful attention to the way we celebrate liturgy, because one of the priceless rewards of the "active participation" (*actuosa participatio*) achieved by the liturgical reform is the careful equilibrium between communal participation and personal interiorization of the liturgy. Authentic participation in the liturgy bears a rhythm, so to speak, of "expression" and "impression," exteriorization and interiorization. One should never be without the other. For this reason, it is necessary always to be on guard for an exaltation of sentiment and emotionalism at the expense of interiorization, spiritual understanding, and personal appropriation of the contents of the liturgy. Easy sentiments and superficial emotions, in the long run, do not nourish the life of faith; only the solid food of the word of God heard and interiorized is the true nourishment of Christian life.

Human awareness and understanding certainly include an affective and emotional component, in which the senses are essentially involved. Indeed, it is through the understanding of the senses that even the liturgy reveals its meaning, for the human person gains awareness of reality and even of the divine mystery only and uniquely through the senses. The senses are a privileged way to meaning. But we must beware of the singular exaltation of sentiments and emotions at the expense of the intellectual and rational component, because the search for pure emotional fulfillment leads to a spectacularist approach to liturgy, seeking the spectacle at all costs, that we often see today. In truth, daily liturgical experience, the daily praying of the psalms, is a challenging and demanding reality. It is often experienced with a dryness that challenges any emotionalism. The great spiritual traditions of both East and the West invite us to discernment, to be wary before the sphere of human emotions, which can be misleading and deceptive. A post-communion prayer with ancient roots reads:

> May the working of this heavenly gift, O Lord, we pray,
> take possession of our minds and bodies,
> so that its effects, and not our own desires,
> may always prevail in us.
> Through Christ our Lord.[25]

The great spiritual guide Brother Roger Schutz, the prior of Taize, wrote: "We must not confuse emotionalism and engagement. I reject emotionalism (but not true and deep emotions). . . . I reject it because my own growth, like that of our community, of the church, and of society, is not dependent on my emotionalism. Engagement, on the other hand, remains very important in many situations."[26]

25. Prayer after Communion, Twenty-fourth Sunday in Ordinary Time, *The Roman Missal, Third Edition* (Collegeville, MN: Liturgical Press, 2011), 484.

26. Roger Schutz, *La tua festa non abbia fine* (Brescia: Morcelliana, 1971), 28.

*Interpretation*

Finally, prayer is an act of interpretation, and in this way, too, liturgy teaches the Christian. Roland Barthes writes, "Listening is a hermeneutical act; to listen means to engage oneself in decoding whatever is obscure, confused, or muted, in order to make what lies beneath the senses appear to the understanding."[27]

If liturgical prayer is interiorized, if the praying person has appropriated for himself the spiritual meaning of the text, he is then able to interpret the text. Interpretation is, most fundamentally, a *symbolic* work, in the sense that the one who prays a psalm must be able to "throw together" (the literal meaning of the Greek root of the word *symbol*), must put-in-relationship the objective meaning of the prayer text and the subjective meaning that the same text provokes in him. A psalm, too, participates in the symbolic nature of liturgical language, because in the context of the liturgy a psalm is also a signifier that awaits to be prayed, awaits the spiritual understanding of the one praying in order to communicate fully its meaning. "The essence of the symbol is to go beyond itself," wrote Marie-Dominique Chenu.[28] Interpretation is the act by which one goes beyond the point of departure that is liturgical prayer, the meaning of which always goes beyond the text.

The liturgical sources provide the impression that the psalms have always been considered a difficult prayer. From the first centuries, the church has provided various auxiliary elements that help believers to pray the psalms as Christians. I refer here above all to three elements still employed today in the praying of the psalms: the *tituli*

27. Barthes and Havas, s.v., "Ascolto," 984.

28. Marie-Dominique Chenu, "Anthropologie et liturgie," *La Maison-Dieu* 12 (1947): 53–65.

*psalmorum*, the antiphons, and the psalm collects. Each of these are tools to facilitate a Christian interpretation of the psalms. They make clear that interpretation is an integral part of Christian prayer and that the one who prays necessarily interprets. On the role of the psalm collect, the General Instruction of the Liturgy of the Hours explains:

> Psalm-prayers for each psalm are given in the supplement to the Liturgy of the Hours, to help in understanding them in a predominantly Christian way. They may be used in the ancient traditional way: after the psalm a period of silence is observed, then the prayer gathers up and rounds off the thoughts and aspirations of those taking part.[29]

The psalm collects are therefore among the instruments with which the liturgy teaches the Christian to pray, forming in him an interpretive ability, offering words about what the praying of the psalm has evoked. It is, in other words, meaningful that the psalm, already in itself prayer, is followed and completed with another prayer text. This reflects all that we have been saying here. The process of listening, interiorization, and interpretation can result in a verbal prayer, like the psalm collect, but it can also manifest itself simply with silent adoration. Through listening, interiorization, and interpretation, the liturgy teaches a kind of prayer that creates in the believer a space of welcome for and communion with the Lord. The liturgy, then, by wise pedagogy, teaches the Christian to go beyond itself and to achieve, through prayer, communion with God.

---

29. General Instruction of the Liturgy of the Hours, n. 112, in *The Liturgy of the Hours*, vol. 1, *Advent Season, Christmas Season* (New York: Catholic Book Publishing, 1975), 60–61.

# Part Three

## A Liturgy
## for the Christianity
## That Lies Ahead of Us

# Chapter Nine

# Liturgy and Love
# for the Poor

*"When you see a believer who is poor . . . remember
that you behold an altar."*

—John Chrysostom[1]

## What Have We Made of the Eucharist?

The relationship between liturgy and solidarity with the poor, between Eucharist and social justice, was a matter of intense discussion and debate within the church during the 1960s and 1970s. This is not so much the case today.[2] Nevertheless, these issues are too much a part of the authentic message of Scripture to treat them simply as passing fads or the fruits of a sincere but misguided idealism that has become less relevant with time. In light of the current economic crisis and all that brought it about, the Christian communities of the West must examine themselves with

1. John Chrysostom, *On the Second Epistle of St. Paul to the Corinthians*, Homily 20.3 (Oxford: John Henry Parker, 1848), 237.
2. This chapter was originally published as *Liturgia e amore per i poveri*, Testi di meditazione 152 (Bose: Qiqajon, 2009).

regard to these topics in order to come to an honest evaluation of the way they have understood and responded to the call to share with the poor that is inherent in the Eucharist.

The relationship between liturgy and poverty cannot be overlooked or ignored. In the pages of both the Old Testament and the New Testament, in the words of the prophets and the wisdom of Israel, in the teaching of Jesus and the preaching of the apostles (and successively in that of the fathers of the church), *the essential quality that makes worship welcome and acceptable to God is that those who offer it also practice justice toward people who are poor, give comfort to people who suffer, and defend the rights of people who are oppressed.* The believer cannot worship the Lord and at the same time ignore the neighbor in need. God does not answer the prayer of one who ignores the cry of the poor, and there can be no authentic worship offered by those who are the cause of injustice.

Since the onset of the economic crisis, we have heard in both the church and the broader society some long-forgotten words, like sobriety, moderation, sharing, self-giving. These words are both authentically evangelical and richly human. Yet Christians cannot ignore the fact that long before the economic crisis began and long after it will have faded into the past, the liturgy calls us to "partake of the table of the Lord" (cf. 1 Cor 10:21) where we are invited to share "one bread" (cf. 1 Cor 10:17) with our sisters and brothers; there can be no communion with God without sharing with one's brothers and sisters. The only authentically Christian koinonia is that which the Lord Jesus demonstrated in the sign of the broken bread given to his disciples. He made clear in this way that in the community of those who follow him, there is no koinonia other than that born of the Eucharist. For this reason, we can say that the breaking of the bread is the most fundamental and essential gesture to the Christian liturgy; we might say that it constitutes the ritual essence of the Eucharist in the same way that the bread is the material substance.

To affirm with *Sacrosanctum Concilium* that the liturgy is the source and summit of the church's life[3] means at the same time to acknowledge that the liturgy is also the source and summit of the ethical life of every Christian community and of every individual believer. We are called by the liturgy itself not to forget our neighbors in need or those living in situations of injustice. The celebration of the Eucharist is not only the *priestly* action of a people called to offer thanksgiving to God for all his gifts in the name of all humanity. It is also the *prophetic* action of a people called to proclaim to all humanity in the name of God the call to share those gifts. In 1971 the bishop Hélder Câmara asked,

> When the Eucharist is received at the moment of death, it is called viaticum; it is nourishment given for the great journey that is about to begin. But what do we call the Eucharist when it is received to nourish our living and our work to make justice live? We must have no illusions: the world knows very well the scandal. That twenty percent of humanity that takes in its hands eighty percent of the goods of the earth are Christians, at least in origins. What have we made of the Eucharist? How can we reconcile it with injustice, the daughter of egoism?[4]

By what name shall we call the Eucharist when it is received to nourish our living and our work to make justice live? There is a good answer to this question posed by Hélder Câmara. Though "viaticum" is indeed one of the traditional names for the Eucharist, a still more ancient name is *klásma*,

---

3. Cf. Second Vatican Council, *Sacrosanctum Concilium*, n. 10.

4. H. Câmara, "L'eucharistie, exigence de justice sociale," *Parole & Pain* 42 (1971): 75–76. The complete text of this article appears below in an appendix to this chapter, on pages 206–8.

"broken," which we find in the *Didache*, written at the dawn of Christianity.[5] The noun *klásma* is commonly understood as a synecdoche that translators render "the bread broken" (equivalent of the expression *tòn árton tòn keklasménom*). The *Didache*, however, by calling the Eucharist simply *klásma*, "broken," intends above all to directly link the piece of bread to the eucharistic gesture that is its origin, the breaking of the single loaf. The *Didache* understands the eucharistic bread not as a subsistent reality in itself as bread (substance) but as bread broken (relation) and made to be shared. In other words, *the eucharistic gesture of "the breaking of the bread" carried out by Jesus himself, the Pauline expression that "all partake of the one bread"* (1 Cor 10:17), *and the name* klásma *given by the* Didache *to the Eucharist all make clear that the sharing of the one bread is the central reality of the Eucharist*. It is not only as bread (substance) but as bread broken and shared (relation), that the eucharistic bread fully realizes its essence and the truth of the Eucharist.

Today more than ever, the *fractio panis* is the great prophetic gesture by which the church proclaims that the Lord has entrusted to humanity the resources of the earth and that those who have abundance must share with the poor in solidarity and justice. The psalmist addressed the Lord:

> The eyes of all look to you,
>    and you give them their food in due season.
> You open your hand,
>    satisfying the desire of every living thing. (Ps 145:15-16)

Hearing this, Christianity insists that no person should suffer hunger, for the goods that God has created for all

---

5. Cf. *Didache* 14.1, in Lawrence J. Johnson, ed., *Worship in the Early Church: An Anthology of Historical Sources*, vol. 1 (Collegeville, MN: Liturgical Press, 2009), 40.

must be shared by all. "Religion that is pure and undefiled before God, the Father, is this: to care for the orphans and widows in their distress," writes the apostle James (1:27), echoing the prophets of Israel. His words remind us that, like the ancient worship, the prophetic and ethical dimension of Christian liturgy, too, is constantly exposed to the danger of being overwhelmed by its priestly dimension. But the purpose of the liturgy is not the believer's sacramentalization but her sanctification. The sacraments of the church, especially baptism and Eucharist, accomplish their full effect by guiding Christians to live as Christ has lived, to "walk just as he walked" (1 John 2:6).

"What have we made of the Eucharist? How can we reconcile it with injustice, the daughter of egoism?" In the economic situation that the West is experiencing, these questions of Hélder Câmara resonate with remarkable relevance. The provocation that these questions contain is not addressed to the world of economics and finance but directly to the church that celebrates the Eucharist, to Christians who are gathered by God every Sunday to break bread and share it with one another. Câmara's pointed questions immediately call to mind earlier questions, just as strongly worded and also born from eucharistic praxis of a Christian community: "Do you not have homes to eat and drink in? Or do you show contempt for the church of God and humiliate those who have nothing?" (1 Cor 11:22). These are the questions that the apostle Paul asked the Christian community of Corinth, which had transformed "the Lord's supper" (1 Cor 11:20) into a meal that was no longer eucharistic and humiliated those who had nothing.

Paul's questions in his first letter to the Corinthians are a source from which every Christian community is called to draw the authentic meaning of its participation in the Lord's Supper and against which they must test their own celebrating and understanding of the Eucharist, because the life of the church and of every Christian flows, for better or worse, from their concrete eucharistic praxis. The difficult question that must therefore be faced is this: Does the economic crisis that the Western nations have experienced perhaps reveal that the eucharistic praxis of the Christian communities that live in them are similar to that of the community of Corinth?

## The Eucharistic Scandal of Corinth

The Christian community of Corinth was very young, founded by Paul himself only four or five years before this letter (see Acts 18:1-18), which the exegetes date around the year 55 (that is, only twenty-five years after the death of Christ). Besides being very young, the community was also small. It numbered a few dozen Christians, maybe fifty, mostly converts from paganism. At the time of Paul, Corinth was a Roman city in the midst of great expansion, in which different cultures, philosophies, styles of life, and religions coexisted. We find these reflected in the religious and social categories that Paul mentions in the letter: "Jews or Greeks, slaves or free" (1 Cor 12:13). From the letter one can deduce that the church in Corinth was composed mostly of persons of the lower-middle class and also of slaves (1 Cor 7:20-24), while a few were rich (1 Cor 11:17-34). With this first letter the apostle Paul confronted and responded to some problems and issues within the community: the divisions, the immorality of some members, the bringing of questions internal to the community before pagan tribunals, the affirmation of the Christian meaning of marriage, the question of eating meat sacrificed to idols, the liturgical assemblies and the way of celebrating the Lord's Supper, and finally, the coordination of the many charisms for the building up of the one church of Christ.

It is quite significant that before addressing these seven problems, Paul first of all proclaims the kerygma, the "message about the cross" (1 Cor 1:18-31), and later concludes the letter by proclaiming the kerygma of the resurrection of Christ (1 Cor 15:51-58). It is as though he wants to say that every difficulty within the Christian community and every moment of crisis in the church find their solution only if confronted by starting from a personal relationship with Christ. We must seek the solutions to the problems the church faces only in Christ and the wisdom of his cross. This is the apostolic teaching of Paul.

## The Lord's Supper

To understand the meaning of the Apostle's criticism, it is necessary to be clear about how the communal meal of the Christians, which Paul called "the Lord's supper," took place. The Christians of Corinth came together regularly in the home of one of their members for this meal. Affluent members of the community who were willing offered their homes for the gathering. They shared what was brought by all who came. Probably the wealthier members brought a lot of rich food and drink, while the less well-off brought what they could. There were also, says Paul, "those who had nothing" to bring. These banquets were quite similar to the pagan banquets of the time but different in two ways. First, there was no distinction made by social class, and every baptized person was welcome to take part. Both the rich and the poor sat together at the same table for the Lord's Supper, including those of very low social conditions, like the slaves. Second, in the course of the meal—we don't know if it happened during the meal or at its conclusion—the Eucharist was celebrated in obedience to the command of Jesus at the Last Supper. A single loaf of bread was broken and each person present ate a piece of it, and a single cup of wine was blessed and each person present took a drink. This is the most ancient form of the Eucharist that is still celebrated by Christians today.

But something had happened to the Lord's Supper in Corinth after his departure from the community:

> [T]o begin with, when you come together as a church, I hear that there are divisions among you; and to some extent I believe it. Indeed, there have to be factions among you, for only so will it become clear who among you are genuine. When you come together, it is not really to eat the Lord's supper. For when the time comes to eat, each of you goes ahead with your own supper, and one goes hungry and another becomes drunk. What! Do you not have homes to eat and drink in? Or do you show contempt for the church of God and humiliate those who have nothing? What should I say to you? Should I commend you? In this matter I do not commend you! (1 Cor 11:18-22)

What happened to Corinth that provoked Paul's criticism? The Apostle had learned that the richest among them were not waiting for all the members and began to eat and drink to the point of getting drunk, leaving poor Christians who came later, maybe because they were busy with work, with nothing to eat. As a result, some were drunk and others were hungry, and regarding this the Apostle observed: "When you come together, it is not really to eat the Lord's supper [*kyriakòn deîpnon*]"; rather, "each of you goes ahead with your own supper [*tò ídion deîpnon*]." John Chrysostom, in a homily on this letter of Paul's, writes with great spiritual understanding about these lines: "The Church was made, not that we who come together might be divided, but that they who are divided might be joined: and this is what the act of assembling shows."[6]

---

6. John Chrysostom, *On the First Epistle of St. Paul to the Corinthians*, Homily 27.4 (Oxford, UK: John Henry Parker, 1848), 375.

In the Christian community of Corinth, the true meaning of Lord's Supper was distorted because a scandalous discrimination—the rich refusing to share their food with the poor—is supported rather than rejected. It is certainly an offense to the believers living in poverty to see so little consideration offered by the rich believers. For this reason, the refusal of the rich to wait for the poor members to celebrate the Lord's Supper with them is not simply lack of courtesy; it is a sign of their contempt. Paul describes this behavior as a "humiliation of those who have nothing," an expression that Jerome in the Vulgate translates as *"Confunditis eum, qui non habent"* (confused and upset, those who have nothing). In his commentary, Chrysostom renders "humiliated" as "made to blush" and observes:

> [Paul] did not say, "You let the poor die of hunger," but he offers a strong word and says, "You make them blush," to point out that it is not food that he cares for so much, as the wrong done to them. Behold again a fifth accusation, not only to overlook the poor, but even to shame them.[7]

## A Liturgy That Humiliates the Poor

Every Christian community that cares about the authenticity of its eucharistic praxis must ask itself: "Are we like the church of Corinth? Do we humiliate those who have nothing by the way we celebrate our liturgy?" The Christians of Corinth failed to recognize the important links between the Eucharist and Christian living. But the liturgy is, in fact, the highest moral act in which a human being can engage, because in it our moral selves are molded by the moral vision of God. In this way, the theophanic experience of the liturgy can become the foundation of every moral choice, because those who celebrate it are able to

7. Ibid.

appropriate for themselves the ethos of the one who "though he was rich, yet for your sakes he became poor" (2 Cor 8:9), the poor one of God who said of himself, "I was hungry and you gave me food, I was thirsty, a stranger, naked, in prison" (see Matt 25:31-46). For this reason, Christian liturgy is the liturgy of the Poor One, that is, a liturgy that manifests an ethic of gift (a body given), an ethic of sharing (one loaf divided among many), an ethic of solidarity and charity (the collection for those in need). It is therefore necessary to recognize that our liturgies are always exposed to the risk of humiliating the poor.

Paul's letters demonstrate a particular attentiveness to sharing with the poor (cf. Rom 15; 2 Cor 8–9; Gal 2:10), promoting among the churches a collection of money for the poor of Jerusalem. In 2 Corinthians, Paul understands the collection as a liturgy and writes: "the rendering of this ministry [*diakonia tes leitourgias*, literally "liturgical service"] not only supplies the needs of the saints but also overflows with many thanksgivings to God" (2 Cor 9:12). In a catechesis on this Pauline text, Pope Benedict XVI interpreted the meaning of the collection: "Love for the poor and the divine liturgy go hand in hand, love for the poor is liturgy. The two horizons are present in every liturgy that is celebrated and experienced in the Church which, by her nature, is opposed to any separation between worship and life, between faith and works, between prayer and charity for the brethren."[8]

In Paul's thought, the collection is not therefore a simple work of comfort and assistance, but, insofar as it is described as "service" and "liturgy," it manifests the mystery

---

8. Pope Benedict XVI, General audience, October 1, 2008, http://www.vatican.va/holy_father/benedict_xvi/audiences/2008/documents/hf_ben-xvi_aud_20081001_en.html, accessed December 8, 2013.

of the church. This explains why, in the praxis of the churches, the collection for the poor of the community took place within the liturgy, as attested to by the apologist Justin in the most ancient description available of a eucharistic celebration:

> [T]hose who prosper, and so wish, contribute what each thinks fit; and what is collected is deposited with the Ruler, who takes care of the orphans and widows, and those who, on account of sickness or any other cause, are in want, and those who are in bonds, and the strangers who are sojourners among us, and in a word [he] is the guardian of all those in need.⁹

The gifts offered by the believers are considered to be offered to the poor and to God; the two destinations form a single act of offering. The unicity of this act is expressed also by the fact that the one who presides over the community's liturgical offering also presides over the community's offering of charity toward the poor. This explains the title *necator pauperum*, "murderer of the poor," which several councils of Gaul during the sixth and seventh centuries used to describe the presbyter who steals from the community's offering.¹⁰

---

9. Justin Martyr, "First Apology 67," *The First and Second Apologies*, trans. Leslie William Barnard, Ancient Christian Writers 56 (New York: Paulist Press, 1997), 71.

10. Cf. Fifth Council of Orléans (549), canons 13, 15, 16, in *Les canons des conciles mérovingiens (VIᵉ-VIIᵉ siecles)*, vol. 1, ed. Jean Gaudemet and Brigitte Basdevant (Paris: Cerf, 1989), 308, 310, 312; Fifth Council of Arles (554), canon 6, ibid., 342; Second Council of Tours (567), canons 25–26, in *Les canons des conciles mérovingiens (VIᵉ-VIIᵉ siecles)*, vol. 2, ed. Jean Gaudemet and Brigitte Basdevant (Paris: Cerf, 1989), 384–88 and others.

It is with the same understanding of charity toward the poor as liturgy that John Chrysostom repeatedly denounced to the Christians of his churches the scandal of nourishing oneself with the body of Christ at the eucharistic table while leaving the poor to die of hunger at the door of the church building. First as bishop of Antioch and later as bishop of Constantinople, he preached with passion against the opulent decoration of the church and vestments of its clergy, insisting that the honor given to Christ in the liturgy can never be separated from the honor given to Christ in the poor. He said, "When you see a believer who is poor . . . remember that you behold an altar."[11]

Chrysostom's thought has resulted in some contemporary authors attributing to him expressions like "sacrament of the neighbor" or "sacrament of the poor," though no such expressions appear in his works. Yet these expressions synthesize well his thinking on the liturgy and love for the poor. That thinking is expressed particularly well in one of his well-known homilies, which may be the most inspired expression of this theme in the history of the church:

> Do you want to honor Christ's body? Do not neglect him when he is naked; do not, while you honor him here with silken garments, neglect Him perishing outside of cold and nakedness. For He that said "This is my body," and by His word confirmed the fact, also said, "You saw me hungry and you did not feed me" and "Whatever you did for one of the least of these, you did for me." This [the body of Christ on the altar] has no need of coverings, but of a pure soul; but that requires much attention. Let us learn therefore to be strict in life, and to honor Christ as He Himself desires. . . .

11. John Chrysostom, *On the Second Epistle of St. Paul to the Corinthians*, Homily 20.3 (Oxford, UK: John Henry Parker, 1848), 237.

For what is the profit, when His table indeed is full of golden cups, but He perishes with hunger? First fill Him, being hungry, and then abundantly deck out His table also. Do you make for Him a cup of gold, while you refuse to give him a cup of cold water? And what is the profit? Do you furnish His table with cloths bespangled with gold, while you refuse Him even the most basic coverings? And what good comes of it?

And these things I say, not forbidding munificence in these matters, but admonishing you to do those other works, together with these, or rather even before these. Because for not having adorned the church no one was ever blamed, but for not having helped the poor, hell is threatened, and unquenchable fire, and the punishment of evil spirits. Do not therefore while adorning His house overlook your brother in distress, for he is more properly a temple than the other.[12]

If love for the poor is liturgy, this is all the more reason for every local church, today more than yesterday, to take great care that its liturgy remains faithful to the liturgical reform of Vatican II, which sought to actuate, in forms and styles, the express will of the council in its Constitution on the Liturgy: "The rites should be distinguished by a noble simplicity."[13] With this statement, we can no longer be misled by the deceit that liturgical styles marked by opulence, pomp, and ostentation are the only way to manifest sacredness and proclaim the splendor of God.

An eighteenth-century author wrote, "Luxury is excessive, but always in flaunting, never in giving."[14] The "noble

12. John Chrysostom, *On the Gospel of St. Matthew*, Homily 50.4 (Oxford, UK: John Henry Parker, 1879), 685–86.

13. Second Vatican Council, *Sacrosanctum Concilium*, n. 34.

14. Giacinto Sigismondo Gerdil, *Discours de la nature et des effets du luxe* (Turin: Frères Reycends, 1768).

simplicity" willed by the council for the liturgy, though, expresses the desire to give, to share. The simplicity of the Christian liturgy is a question of ethics and, as such, also of theology. The liturgy is, in fact, *opus Dei*; it is the action of God through Christ in the Holy Spirit. For this reason, in the liturgy, form is substance! While Jesus' style of acting is never to "humiliate those who have nothing," the liturgy of Corinth humiliates the poor, excluding them from the abundance of the rich.

If there can be a way of celebrating the Eucharist that excludes the poor, there is also a way of celebrating it in which the poor are not excluded but feel welcome and comfortable, because their human and Christian dignity is recognized. "[Y]ou have dishonored the poor," admonished the apostle James (Jas 2:6), reminding his community that in the liturgical assembly every baptized person must be welcomed for his belonging to Christ and not based on his social belonging and economic condition:

> [I]f a person with gold rings and in fine clothes comes into your assembly, and if a poor person in dirty clothes also comes in, and if you take notice of the one wearing the fine clothes and say, "Have a seat here, please," while to the one who is poor you say, "Stand there," or, "Sit at my feet," have you not made distinctions among yourselves, and become judges with evil thoughts? Listen, my beloved brothers and sisters. Has not God chosen the poor in the world to be rich in faith and to be heirs of the kingdom that he has promised to those who love him? But you have dishonored the poor. (Jas 2:2-6)

The *Didascalia Apostolorum* even goes beyond James in its instructions for the liturgical assembly when it calls for the bishop to interrupt his own preaching in order to be personally attentive to the poor who arrive in the assembly, to find them a place to sit, even at the cost of giving them his own episcopal cathedra:

> If . . . when you are seated, some other man or woman should arrive who is honoured in the world, whether from the same district or from some other congregation, you should not, bishop, leave off your ministry of the word, whether you are speaking of it, or hearing it, or reading, in order to show them to a place, but remain as you are and do not interrupt the word. Rather the brothers should themselves receive them. . . . But if a poor man or woman should arrive, whether from the same district or from another congregation, most especially if they are well on in years, and they have no place, then you, bishop, should act for them from your heart, even should you sit on the ground yourself. There should be no respect of persons with you, but you should please God, through your ministry.[15]

These descriptions of the Christian liturgical assembly as the place where the poor must be welcomed, recognized, and even honored are the exact opposite of what Paul knew to be happening in the eucharistic suppers at Corinth. Such a welcoming is certainly not limited to making sure everyone has a place to sit; it must also be expressed in the style of the celebration itself. It must be a simple and, above all, noble style that proclaims the beauty of God without humiliating the poor for their poverty. To speak of a simple liturgy does not mean to permit a liturgy that is in any way sloppy, neglected, and therefore inexpressive; this is a pauperism that is certainly not Christian in nature. The simple

---

15. *The Didacalia Apostolorum: An English Version*, chap. 12, trans. Alistair Stewart-Sykes (Turnhout, Belgium: Brepols, 2009), 176–77.

beauty of the liturgy must rather be sought with great effort and care. Such simplicity is always a goal and never a starting point, because it means searching for that pure and essential nucleus of each thing, whether it be a material or fabric but also a word, a gesture, an image, a sound, a song. It is much easier to settle for beauty through the pageantry, sumptuousness, and luxury, which are the worldly forms of beauty. Worldly beauty is an anesthetic beauty that fixes our eyes only on the object, which means we close the eyes to the world, to others, and to reality.[16] The beauty of the liturgy, though, is not an anesthetic beauty; it is a beauty that makes of the object a simple sign that invites us to open our ears to the word of God and to open our eyes wide to others and to reality. For this reason, the simple beauty of the Christian liturgy is not a worldly beauty but a holy beauty, because it reflects the beauty of God and the beauty to which every person is called.

While some in this time of economic crisis irresponsibly preach more consumption, the church is called to witness to the value of "forgotten sobriety,"[17] first of all in its liturgy, which, of all that is hers, may be most immediately visible even to the eyes of nonbelievers.

### *"Memoria Passionis"*

Paul insists that it is possible to celebrate a liturgical rite but fail to celebrate the Supper of the Lord, a supper in which Jesus Christ is the Lord, in which the table is the

---

16. Cf. Maurilio Assenza, Giovanni Salonia, and Antonio Sichera, "Povertà e bellezza," in M. Assenza, Luca Licitra, Giovanni Salonia, Antonio Sichera, *Lo sguardo dal basso. I poveri come principio del pensare* (Ragusa: Argo, 2002), 27–57.

17. Cf. Dionigi Tettamanzi, *La sobrietà dimenticata* (Milan: Centro Ambrosiano, 2009).

table of the Lord. Responding to this situation in Corinth, the Apostle recalls Jesus' last supper with his disciples:

> I received from the Lord what I also handed on to you, that the Lord Jesus on the night when he was betrayed took a loaf of bread, and when he had given thanks, he broke it and said, "This is my body that is for you. Do this in remembrance of me." In the same way he took the cup also, after supper, saying, "This cup is the new covenant in my blood. Do this, as often as you drink it, in remembrance of me." For as often as you eat this bread and drink the cup, you proclaim the Lord's death until he comes. (1 Cor 11:23-26)

Though Paul was not present himself at the vigil of the passion when Jesus entrusted this sign to the twelve, he speaks of the Eucharist as something that he received from the Lord himself and he has faithfully, in his turn, transmitted to the community of Corinth, attesting to how the apostolic tradition must protect and transmit the Eucharist in its essential form. Paul has simply transmitted what he received; he has not invented anything. The words spoken by Jesus in Paul's account differ from those in the synoptics in the expression "body that is for you" (*tò sôma tò hypèr hymôn*), literally "body-for-you." This expression suggests that a fundamental relationship is written into the body of Jesus. It is not simply *body* but is in essence *body-for-you*, body given; the gift-nature of Jesus' body is not added in a second moment but belongs to it from the start. The Eucharist is the memorial of Jesus' *body-for-you*, and it is by holding the eucharistic praxis of the church in Corinth up to this criteria that Paul judges this community. It is also the measure by which every eucharistic liturgy must be judged. *Body-for-you* means body given, handed over, life spent fully, life offered for others. The *body-for-you* negates every individualistic logic similar to that of the rich in the community of Corinth. Every egoism, every spirit of division is refuted by the mutual welcoming and total sharing that characterizes the full communion that is the Eucharist. Chrysostom asked:

> Why remember the institution of the holy mysteries? Why in this moment is it necessary to recall [the Last Supper]? Your Lord, [Paul] wants to say, deigned to welcome you all to his banquet, though it is holy and venerable, and you, meanwhile, dare to judge the poor to be unworthy of your miserable little table.[18]

Chrysostom's response offers a key to understanding Paul's point. Paul reminds the Corinthians, who in the Lord's Supper did not share their bread with the poor, judging them unworthy of their table, that Christ instituted the Eucharist as a *memoria passionis,* a memorial of a life not grasped on to but given, not saved by one but offered for the salvation of all. Paul insisted that a Christian cannot think of participating in the Eucharist, making memorial of the Last Supper, if he lives the logic of his own supper (*tò ídion deîpnon*), of his own life. A person who, though Christian, lives a logic of saving his own life, regardless of others, sooner or later will live against others and at the expense of others. One who lives only for herself, for her own interests and her own success, will also eat the body of the Lord for herself and not for others, not in communion. No Christian community or person can live such an individual logic—be it ecclesial or existential—without turning away from a logic of communion, a logic of *body-for-you,* the exact opposite of the logic of *body-for-me.* Inasmuch as a Christian is a member of the church, the logic of *for-you,* the logic of koinonia, must be given primacy in

---

18. John Chrysostom, *Commentary on the First Letter to the Corinthians,* 27.3. [My translation from the Italian.—Trans.]

personal and communal life. Only in this way can we celebrate the Eucharist as a *memoria passionis*, repeating the
words of Jesus: "This is my *body-for-you*."

Basil, bishop of Caesarea and father of the church,
asked:

> What is proper of the one who eats the bread and drinks
> the cup of the Lord? To guard the ongoing memorial of
> the one who died and rose for us. What is proper of the
> one that guards this memorial? To live no longer for one-
> self, but for him who died and rose for us.[19]

As the Christian, nourished by the Eucharist, becomes
guardian of the "ongoing memorial of the one who died
and rose," he also becomes himself a memorial of the Passover of Christ.

## To Eat and Drink One's Condemnation

To speak of the Lord's Supper calls to mind the great
apostolic admonition of Paul:

> Whoever, therefore, eats the bread or drinks the cup of the
> Lord in an unworthy manner will be answerable for the
> body and blood of the Lord. Examine yourselves, and only
> then eat of the bread and drink of the cup. For all who eat
> and drink without discerning the body, eat and drink judg-
> ment against themselves. For this reason many of you are
> weak and ill, and some have died. (1 Cor 11:27-30)

Those who do not discern the body of the Lord "eat and
drink judgment against themselves," Paul says in words

---

19. Basil of Caesarea, *Regole morali* 80.22. [My translation from
the Italian.—Trans.]

that inspire fear and call for great vigilance by anyone who celebrates the Eucharist. But what does it mean to discern the body and the blood of the Lord? Certainly Paul means first of all that to participate in the Eucharist means to discern in faith that the bread broken is the body of the Lord and that the wine drunk is his blood.

But to discern the body of the Lord also means, for Paul, a second discernment: to discern the holy reality of the church as the body of Christ. This second discernment is also one of faith, and often the ecclesial discernment is more difficult and demanding than the sacramental. It means to be aware that one's brothers and sisters make up the body of Christ, members of a single body of the Lord in a unity that is always a work of the Holy Spirit. The mystery of the church and the mystery of the Eucharist form a single mystery to such an extent that only one who understands the Eucharist knows what the church is, and only one who knows the profound reality of the church can understand the Eucharist. This is why Paul says it is impossible to fail to discern the ecclesial body and to think of communicating worthily in the eucharistic body. The Apostle demands that the Christians of Corinth ask themselves about their gathering in assembly; they don't wait for one another and so remain divided, because they are not aware of being gathered uniquely by Christ and with the death of Christ in mind.

The dynamism of gathering is certainly essential for the Eucharist and therefore for the Christian community, but we are not talking simply about a web of strategic or functional human ties. In the church it is not enough to be together for a common purpose. Rather, the Lord Jesus alone is the profound reason for being and acting as church. In the church there are no specially chosen members like the rich of Corinth considered themselves to be; the church is not an exclusive club or a private circle, an association based on social status, culture, political ideas, interests, or hobbies. The church is gathered by God and by God alone; one is called to be a part of it through the gift of faith. "To discern the body of the Lord" is the admonition offered to every believer. We must discern the nature of our own Christian communities, asking whether they are based on affective, psychological, and therefore purely carnal relationships. Often Christian communities are marked by divisions that are not so much social as affective; they develop based on human sympathies and sometimes on interests opposed to the Gospel that in fact exclude others. The Lutheran theologian Dietrich Bonhoeffer described such exclusions like this:

> When the way of intellectual or spiritual selection is taken the human element always insinuates itself and robs the fellowship of its spiritual power and effectiveness for the Church, drives it into sectarianism. The exclusion of the weak and insignificant, the seemingly useless people, from a Christian community may actually mean the exclusion of Christ; in the poor brother Christ is knocking at the door.[20]

If love for the Lord Jesus is not the only reason for gathering and living as the church of God, sooner or later the other reasons surface and reveal themselves as a source of exclusion and division within the Christian community.

The Apostle prophetically admonishes us that the Eucharist is not only good news but also judgment when he writes that "all who eat and drink without discerning the body, eat and drink judgment against themselves. For this reason many of you are weak and ill, and some have died"

---

20. Dietrich Bonhoeffer, *Life Together*, trans. John W. Doberstein (New York: Harper and Row, 1954), 37–38.

(1 Cor 11:29-30). In the community of Corinth, because of the failure to discern the body of the Lord, many were fragile, weak, sick, and dying. A terrible justice is unleashed by the Eucharist when one fails to recognize brothers and sisters in Christ, when one excludes one's neighbors and refuses to share one's spiritual and material goods. Then the Eucharist becomes judgment and members eat and drink judgment against themselves. If the life of a Christian community today is marked by weakness, exhaustion, or suffering, perhaps it is because its way of celebrating the Eucharist reveals an incapacity to discern the sacramental and ecclesial body of Christ.

Paul tells the Christians of Corinth that when we are nourished by the Eucharist, we never remain as we were before but are always transformed, for better or worse. Just as the word of God is always living and efficacious (cf. Heb 4:12-13), so also are the sacraments, especially the Eucharist, which always produces its effect, never leaving the one who is nourished by it as she was before. Either the person conforms herself in her life to the gift of grace received, or refusing it she aggravates the situation of sin, in Pauline terms, eats and drinks judgment against herself. The Apostle rejects any sacramental automatism, because the Eucharist, like the word of God, bears a power that, when distorted in meaning or contradicted in fact, does not remain neutral but leaves one spiritually weak and infirm.

### *Yours Is an Eating of the Lord's Supper*

We conclude this reflection by turning Paul's criticism of the Corinthian community into a positive exhortation: "When you come together, it is to eat the Lord's supper!" Paul's Greek text uses a very important expression: "When you gather *epì tò autó*" is translated above as "when you come together," but it literally means "when you gather in yourself." To say that believers gather "in themselves" means much more than saying they are simply together in the same place. To be gathered *epì tò autó* means a gathering in the unity that is given by Jesus Christ and by no other. It is not a unity born of the will or desire of those who gather but by the love of Christ that each of them has.

"*Congregavit nos in unum Christi amor*," says an ancient Gregorian chant. If it is the believers' love of Christ that gathers them *in unum*, then only those who celebrate the liturgy as an act of love of the poor Christ can also live and understand the liturgy as love of people who are poor. For Christians, sharing goods with the poor is therefore not only a question of social justice; it is also a christological question and consequently a sacramental question. What was true of the community of Corinth is also true of Christian communities of today: not to share with one's poorest neighbors "show[s] contempt for the church of God" (1 Cor 11:22).

All of this leads us to observe that the central issue for Christians today is to believe in the church as communion, as body of Christ. In a culture marked by individualism, competition, affirmation of oneself at all costs, even at the expense of others and against others, it is difficult to be church, to truly be a community. Only from the Eucharist, from the prophetic gesture of the breaking of the bread, can the Christian communities of the West renew their awareness that the church cannot be the body of Christ where Christians fail to turn away from egoism and refuse to share their goods with the poor.

Until the Christian communities of the Western world live their eucharistic liturgy as the presentation to God of the bread that is "fruit of the earth and work of human hands" and share it in the presence of God with their brothers and sisters, they will always be in some way responsible for that social injustice that is at the origins of the economic crisis, because that which is not shared with others in communion is taken from others in injustice.

According to Sirach, God does not like a sacrifice that is the fruit of injustice toward the poor, because

> Like one who kills a son before his father's eyes
> is the person who offers a sacrifice form the property of
>     the poor. (Sir 34:24)

## The Eucharist, a Call to Social Justice[21]
### Hélder Câmara

When the Christian community participates in the Eucharist, at the moment of the offertory it sees in the hands of the celebrant the bread which is "fruit of the earth and work of human hands," and it receives a lesson in the social justice that must mark our lives. How can we not think at that moment that the bread that is set before us is also the fruit of money and that millions of people—two-thirds of the world—have no bread?

Throughout the celebration of the Eucharist, we say that we are brothers and sisters, and we pray to a common Father. We gather around the same table and we nourish ourselves of the same bread of life. And yet after Mass, each of us returns to our own families, our own preoccupations and problems, and these so-called brothers and sisters are forgotten, or worse, they become our adversaries or enemies.

---

21. Presented here is the complete text of Hélder Câmara's article, "L'eucharistie, exigence de justice sociale." (See n. 4 above.) [My translation from the Italian.—Trans.]

When we receive Communion, the eucharistic presence is brief, but it intensifies the union with Christ that began at our baptism. If we are one with Christ, how can we see, without profound sadness, the horrible consequences of egoism on persons, families, communities, nations, and the world? How can we remain indifferent to the growth of injustice and, consequently, the increase of radicalization and hate? By nourishing ourselves with the Eucharist, we are immersed ever more deeply in Christ and linked ever more tightly to all of humanity, and so we must be present to humanity as Christ is. Seeing with the eyes of Christ, how can we fail to recognize that it is not enough in our day to give alms and to call for generosity toward those who are hungry? Today, true alms is to promote justice and to work for social justice.

In our age, the poor are not only individuals and groups; they make up entire countries and continents. The reasons for this poverty—which has millions of God's children living in misery and subhuman conditions—are grave injustices created by the international politics of trade.

From the bread of life, one must draw the strength to allow a change of mentality, an upsetting of our lives, conversion. This means more than trying to understand some complex and difficult arguments, for that is much easier than to work for basic reforms or, more precisely, for structural changes.

We have to open ourselves to divine grace so that in doing justice, we never forget charity; in accepting justice, we demonstrate by God's grace that, in the Eucharist, it is not bread that we receive, it is not a shadow that we embrace, but it is truly the living Christ who is present.

When the Eucharist is received at the moment of death, it is called viaticum; it is nourishment given for the great journey that is about to begin. But what do we call the Eucharist when it is received to nourish our living and our work to make justice live? We must have no illusions: the world knows very well the scandal. The twenty percent of humanity that takes in its hands eighty percent of the goods of the earth are Christians, at least in origins. What have we made of the Eucharist? How can we reconcile it with injustice, the daughter of egoism?

"Go be reconciled to your brother or sister, and then come to the Eucharist" (cf. Matt 5:24). Understanding this word of Christ, do we experience at times some remorse of conscience? We who receive Communion are seen and judged. Those who do not have faith or who have fallen away from religious practice want to discover, from the effects that Communion has in us, whether the Eucharist is only bread or if there is in us some mysterious strength that goes beyond human capacities.

How many times have we already taken Communion? How many times have we already participated in the mystery of the death and resurrection and the Son of God? All that remains, then, is to make a sincere effort and, relying on divine grace, to be credible witnesses of the Eucharist.

In the early days of the church, the pagans were struck by how those who received the bread of life loved one another—not in a theoretical way or only with words, but in practical ways, with actions. The world needs our witness again, so that it may know that the Eucharist compels us to live justice and love as the only ways to true peace.

# Chapter Ten

# Liturgy and the Transmission of the Faith

*"The liturgy is a great thing. It is the most important organ of the ordinary magisterium of the church."*

—Pius XI[1]

One result of the liturgy's vital relationship with the sacred Scriptures is that the liturgy is a primary source of the Christian faith; it contains and expresses the most constitutive elements of that faith.[2] If the church believes what it prays, then every liturgy is a profession of faith. In particular, every eucharistic celebration is the highest profession of faith. The faith of Christians is expressed in a fundamental way in the eucharistic prayer. There is, then, an indissoluble link between the liturgy and the transmission of the faith. We can say, in fact, that the celebration of the liturgy is the most important act of evangelization

1. Cited in Bernard Capelle, "Le Saint Siège et le movement liturgique," *Les Questions Liturgiques et Paroissiales* 3 (1936): 134.
2. This chapter was originally published as *Liturgia e transmissione della fede oggi*, Testi di meditazione 143 (Bose: Qiqajon, 2008).

we can carry out. As Pius XI taught: "The liturgy is a great thing. It is the most important organ of the ordinary magisterium of the church."

From many directions today, there are signs that suggest a gradual but real flowering of a new awareness of the decisive role played by liturgy in the transmission of the faith. For several years the churches of the West have been aware that recent decades have been marked by a certain failure in the transmission of the Christian faith. Among the generations that lived through the decisive period of the council and those that that followed after it, we have seen a breakdown in the transmission of the essential contents of the faith. This explains, at least in part, the choice by many local churches in recent years to be more attentive to religious formation and education, especially of the young. We are now, it is clear, more aware of the difficulty of transmitting the faith and, at the same time, of the necessity of going about it anew, with methods that are more effective within the circumstances of our own day.

My reflections below, on liturgy and the way it transmits the Christian faith, come in three parts:

1. how the liturgy transmits the faith today
2. how the liturgy has always transmitted the faith
3. how the liturgy will transmit the faith tomorrow

### How the Liturgy Transmits the Faith Today

We begin by considering the perspective offered by the Italian bishops in their pastoral plan for the first decade of the new millennium, which was titled "Communicating the Gospel in a World of Change." With that decade now past, it is possible to reread this text in the light of the lived experience of the church. The thoughtful judgment of the Italian bishops was that the transmission of the true meaning of the liturgy was one of the most difficult problems faced by the church in Italy. It is not difficult to see this problem within the wider context of the problem of transmitting the faith, which, as we have said, happens in an important way through the liturgy. Insofar as it is offered by a national bishops' conference, this evaluation is important and bears an indisputable authority. As we move past the first decade of the twenty-first century, this text offers a helpful assessment of the situation.

We read in this pastoral plan:

> Despite the great benefits of the liturgical reform of the Second Vatican Council, one of today's most difficult problems is the transmission of the true meaning of the Christian liturgy. We find a certain lethargy within the church and with it the temptations either to return to old formalisms or to venture off in a naïve search for the spectacular. It appears, sometimes, that the sacramental event is forgotten. From here comes the urgency of making clear the relevance of the *liturgy* as an *educative and revelatory* event, making clear its dignity and its orientation toward the building up of the Kingdom. Such a eucharistic celebration demands much of the priest who presides over the assembly and calls for a robust liturgical formation of the faithful. It demands a liturgy that is at the same time serious, simple, and beautiful, one that conveys mystery but is at the same time intelligible, able to narrate the perennial covenant of God with humanity.[3]

The Italian bishops observe first of all that, despite the good that resulted from the liturgical reform, one of the

3. Conferenza Episcopale Italiana, *Comunicare il vangelo in un mondo che cambia*, n. 49. Text of this document available at http://www.chiesacattolica.it/cci_new/pagine/1653/Notiziario%205_2001 .pdf, accessed December 18, 2013.

biggest problems in the church today is "the transmission of the true meaning of the Christian liturgy." This especially concerns the younger generations, to whom the meaning of the liturgy has not been adequately transmitted. We must carefully examine the so-called youth ministry carried out in recent decades. What did we teach the young, if not the true meaning of Christian liturgy? Given that prayer is the first act of faith, what quality is there to any evangelization that does not teach the meaning of the liturgy? Finally, what kind of liturgies have we been celebrating if we have failed to communicate the very meaning of the liturgy itself? The true meaning of the liturgy, in fact, is not transmitted principally by way of teaching about the liturgy; rather, it is acquired primarily by regular participation in the liturgy, Sunday after Sunday, in the Christian community to which one belongs.

### The Temptation to Return to Old Formalisms

As a direct consequence of our failure to transmit the true meaning of the liturgy to young people, the Italian bishops discern "a certain lethargy" in our liturgies. This lethargy manifests itself in a sense of routine, doing it because it must be done, but without conviction or passion. One reaction to this lethargy among the young is, it seems to the bishops, the temptation to "return to old formalisms" that the liturgical reform had intended to help us overcome.

Often the young—and among them especially those who have a particular interest in and passion for the liturgy (seminarians and novices, for example)—seem to have nostalgia for a past they never knew, for the simple reason that they never lived it. They have nostalgia for the liturgy that earlier generations struggled with because it was carried out in an incomprehensible language, far from their needs. With the coming of the conciliar liturgical reform, those earlier generations were happy to leave behind that liturgy without the slightest regret. The temptation to re-turn to old formalisms appears as a sign not only that something essential is missing in the transmission and the reception of the conciliar liturgical reform but above all that something today is getting in the way of living, cele-brating, and understanding the liturgy. If the liturgy is not well lived, celebrated, and understood, one's life is in some way damaged and dented. One who desires the past is unsatisfied with the present and receives little from the current way of celebrating the liturgy. Perhaps the rites were renewed, but the way of living and understanding the liturgy remained preconciliar. We might therefore apply to the liturgy an observation from the rabbinical tradition: "For God it was easier to get the Jews out of Egypt than to get Egypt out of the Jews."

## The Naïve Search for the Spectacular

The bishops recognize as a second temptation that comes in reaction to the lethargy that afflicts the liturgy that of "ventur[ing] off in a naïve search for the spectacular," the temptation to see the liturgy as spectacle, a phenomenon of attraction, preoccupation, and exaltation. The purpose of the spectacular is to stir up strong emotions and intense sensations, to exalt the emotions at the expense of interior-ity, rationality, thought, silence, and above all a simplicity of the actions and signs that have marked Christian liturgy from the beginning: a piece of bread, a sip of wine, the usual people of my community, my priest, my local church and the liturgy it celebrates—none of these are considered to be spectacular. We have to ask whether the young have perhaps become—year after year, international youth day after international youth day, national rally after national rally, event after event—too habituated to massive liturgies, emotional and exultant, that are certainly Christian in sub-stance but not in style or form. A liturgy that is spectacular enchants the eyes of everyone but converts the hearts of no one. In Christianity, what is essential is and remains invisible to the eyes.

Although we have received some wonderful fruits of the liturgical reform, the Italian bishops recognized that within the current situation of the church, there has been a failure to transmit the true meaning of the liturgy. The real risks are formalism and spectacle, while the way ahead is a rediscovery of the seriousness, simplicity, and beauty of the liturgy. We must rediscover these three characteristics so that the younger generations and those who follow them might be able to know the true meaning of Christian liturgy and, by means of this, to know the mystery of faith.

## How the Liturgy Has Always Transmitted the Faith

We have been speaking about the liturgy; now the liturgy itself will speak. Among many possible examples of how the liturgy transmits the faith, we offer two:

1. liturgy transmits faith in the mystery of the church
2. liturgy transmits faith in the mystery of the Eucharist

Both of these examples demonstrate that liturgy does not transmit the faith through discourses on the truths to be believed but through transforming what is believed into ritual action.

### Liturgy's Transmission of Faith in the Mystery of the Church

When we confess our faith by reciting the Creed, we say, "I believe in one, holy, catholic, and apostolic church." The liturgy has its own distinct way of making real for the believer its faith in the church. This is not done with theological concepts or doctrinal formulas proper to the other aspects of Christian life, like theological reflection or catechetical lessons. It happens by making the church alive, by touching the church with one's hands and plunging into it. The liturgy, in other words, does not *describe* the church but allows it to be *experienced* in the concrete liturgical assembly of the Christian community to which one belongs. Each person steps into the Sunday liturgical assembly, made up of regular people who are neither better nor worse than one another. Some are known well among those gathered, others are completely unknown; the only thing that all have in common is being in the same place at the same moment to carry out the most fundamental act of the Christian faith: hearing the word of God, breaking the bread, drinking from the cup. It is not our personal familiarity with one another that unites us; our communion is born from that which together is received by those who make up this holy assembly.

Faith makes the believer aware that the concrete gathering of the faithful is a true manifestation of the holy church of God, made up of people of various ages, social conditions, levels of culture, and political convictions. It is often clear that some people seated beside each other humanly have nothing in common. And yet this assembly, comprised of people so different from one another, is a reflection not only of the church in abstract but of the Christian community that one has perhaps known and belonged to for decades. This community, which in its ordinary life is often marked by divisions and wounds, is the epiphany of the body of Christ. It is called to be one body, to receive the gift of koinonia. The more koinonia seems to us to be completely out of reach in human terms, the more clearly it is the freely given gift of God. Human abilities alone, even the most elevated, are not enough to bring about sacred koinonia. It is the fruit of the Holy Spirit who pours the love of God into the hearts of believers (see Rom 5: 5). *"Congregavit nos in unum Christi amor,"* proclaims an ancient chant. The love of Christ gathers us and makes us one.

Just before the distribution of Communion, the liturgy invites us to exchange a sign of peace with our brothers and sisters in faith, many of whose names we often do not even know. The peace that Christians offer each other is a divine gift, never simply the fruit of personal sentiments or feelings. The brother with whom I exchange peace is a symbol of the person whom I most need to forgive and the person from whom I hope to receive forgiveness. That is why every excess and euphoria are out of place in the liturgy's exchange of peace, which too often becomes exaggerated and out of control. This is not the moment to introduce oneself and exchange greetings but to give pardon and seek pardon. To say to one another, "Peace be with you," means to recognize in each other the need for and the gift of forgiveness. Within the logic of the liturgy, the two or three people standing near me with whom I exchange peace become in that moment the sign of the concrete person with whom I recently reconciled or with whom I hope to reconcile soon. In that gesture of peace, I express my openness to peace and reconciliation, received first of all from God and then given and received in everyday life. I receive, so to speak, a mandate that I am called to make a part of my daily living. I receive the gift of peace that I am called to give and to know that I have received. The truth of the sign of peace will therefore be linked to the sobriety and the care with which I express it within the liturgy. If I exchange peace in a superficial and thoughtless way, running the risk of banalizing so great a gift, it may mean that I also live it out in a superficial and thoughtless way. If I exchange peace with all, in reality I give it to no one, in the rite and in life.

What the constitution *Lumen Gentium* says about the life of the church in general, we can say in a particular way of the liturgy:

> [The] Church of Christ is really present in all legitimately organized local groups of the faithful . . . united to their pastors. . . . In these communities, though they may often be small and poor, or existing in the diaspora, Christ is present through whose power and influence the One, Holy, Catholic, and Apostolic Church is constituted.[4]

"Small and poor" communities sometimes (but fortunately do not always) offer a liturgy that is "small and poor" in terms of beauty, harmony, and order. The French liturgist Louis-Marie Chauvet has described well the temptation faced by many of the faithful, especially those given to a certain aesthetic, musical, or artistic sense, who are troubled by the quality of the liturgical celebration:[5] "My parish is not beautiful. The church is ugly, the cantor sings poorly, the priest's homilies are banal, the children are noisy, and so on. Am I not perhaps more united to God when I watch the Mass on television at home? Sitting in front of the television, I pray better!" The response of the church is clear: "It is to your parish assembly that God calls you, even if it is less beautiful than the Mass on television." Why? Because that concrete assembly, where you encounter people whom you have not chosen, teaches you what the church is. The church is not a club made up of friends who enjoy spending time together, and the liturgy is not a musical concert (although singing and music of high quality is important). In the assembly of the church, we do not gather in the name

4. Second Vatican Council, *Lumen Gentium*, n. 26.
5. Louis-Marie Chauvet, "Pratique sacramentelle et expérience chrétienne," *Christus* 171 (1996): 275–87, esp. 280–87.

of human affections and friendships; rather, we gather "in the name of the Father, and of the Son, and of the Holy Spirit." It is no coincidence that the eucharistic celebration begins with this Trinitarian formula. Each time, it reminds those who gather that the church is not a gathering of people of our own choosing but the gathering of men and women whom God, and no one else, has called to himself.

The liturgical assembly is a great school of humanity. Certainly, one can and must hope that the songs are beautiful, that the homilies are good (or at least short!), and that the children are quiet. But shortcomings like these are simply part of the human condition. The concrete assembly, and not some ideal that does not exist, is the holy church of God, the body of Christ, the temple of the Holy Spirit, and at the same time is a fully human assembly. The church is holy not despite its humanity but at the heart of its humanity—that humanity that God in Christ came to seek and sanctify in the Spirit. This is how the liturgy transmits the church's faith in its own nature. The liturgy says to us, in a sense: "Do you want to know, to learn, to guard, and to transmit the mystery of the church? Take part in your parish liturgical assembly, and there you will learn what the church is, what the body of Christ is. As long as you have not included and accepted this parish assembly in your definition of the church, you have not included or accepted fully the mystery of the church, because here you encounter, you come to know, that humanity for which Christ has given his life."

Every doctrine *about* the church must therefore be preceded by an experience *of* the church, lived and practiced *in* the church as it is encountered in the ordinary life of a particular community. Only the person who chooses and accepts living the real, local Sunday eucharistic assembly, never taking flight in search of some happy island of a special religious movement or community, can ever truly come to know the real church. Even the monastic liturgy, because of its special characteristics, can often appear more attractive than a parish liturgy, yet it can in no way represent a stable or ordinary substitution for the Sunday eucharistic assembly of the Christian community to which one belongs.

In sum, the liturgy is the first and fundamental school of the mystery of the church and its humanity. This is what it means to transmit the faith: not ideals or notions, but the wisdom of the human things inspired by God. This nonintellectual awareness of the mystery of God and the church comes only through a full awareness of reality, learning from the situations and events around us. Bernard of Clairvaux wrote to a novice: "Believe me who have experience, you will find much more labouring amongst the woods than you ever will amongst books. Woods and stones will teach you what you can never hear from any master."[6]

## *Liturgy's Transmission of Faith in the Mystery of the Eucharist*

A bit of mystagogical reflection on a particular action carried out by the faithful during the liturgy—the rite of Communion—will help us consider the way the liturgy transmits the church's faith regarding the mystery of the Eucharist. Why does the liturgy ask each of us, in order to receive the Eucharist, to get up from where we are located during the celebration, to join a brief procession with our fellow worshipers, to open our hands to receive the eucharistic bread, and to respond "Amen" to the minister who says "The Body of Christ"? Through this sacramental sequence made up of simple gestures and words, the liturgy transmits the faith of the church in the Eucharist.

---

6. *The Letters of St. Bernard of Clairvaux*, Letter 107, trans. Bruno Scott James (Kalamazoo, MI: Cistercian Publications, 1998), 156.

The rite expects that the faithful do not receive the Eucharist at their seats but that they are called to leave their places and walk toward the altar. In this way, the liturgy invites the faithful to carry out a movement, a walk that manifests that the Eucharist is bread for the *homo viator*, the journeying person. The Eucharist is indeed the viaticum, the bread for the voyage, just as the manna was for the people of Israel and as bread was for the prophet Elijah.

The believer does not make her journey alone but only together with brothers and sisters in faith; this is expressed in the Communion procession, which therefore becomes a sign. Here the liturgy teaches me that this is not only my condition but also the condition of all Christians. The church is a people on journey toward the Kingdom. It is helpful to recall that *synodus* ("journey together") is one of the most ancient names for the Christian liturgical assembly.[7]

The Communion procession is therefore the image of humanity on the way toward God, each of us in our own circumstances and states of life. All go together toward the altar, each of us as we are, with our own particular burdens of misery and sin, our labors, all compelled by the same hunger to receive the bread of forgiveness, the bread of mercy, the bread of eternal life that only God can give. In his *Resuscitare*, the French writer Christian Bobin describes in a suggestive way the Communion procession of a group of the faithful at a Mass on Easter morning, recognizing in it a vision of the resurrection to come:

> At the moment of communion, at the Easter Mass, the people got up in silence, walked down the side aisles to the back of the church, then turned one by one up the

---

7. Cf. the texts cited in Goffredo Boselli, " 'Convenire in unum'. L'assemblea liturgica nei testi del Concilio: due nodi ancora irrisolti," *La Rivista del Clero Italiano* 3 (2008): 165–86.

central aisle, advancing to the front, where they received the host from a bearded priest with silver-rimmed glasses, helped by two women with faces hardened by the importance of their role, the kind of ageless women who change the flowers on the altar before they wilt and take care of God like he was a tired old husband. Seated at the back of the church, waiting my turn to join the procession, I looked at the people, their postures, their backs, their necks, the profiles of their faces. For a second my view opened and I saw all of humanity, its millions of individuals, included in this slow and silent flow: old and adolescent, rich and poor, adulterous women and earnest girls, crazies, killers, and geniuses, all scraping their shoes on the cold, rough stone tiles of the church floor, like the dead who will rise patiently from their darkness to go and receive the light. Then I understood what the resurrection will be like and the stunning calm that will precede it.[8]

Standing before the minister, the faithful carry out a simple but intense gesture, raising their arms and opening their hands to receive the eucharistic bread. They open their hands as people about to receive a gift, and this gesture reveals an interior attitude. It is an act of the spirit. To open one's hands is the purest human gesture one can make to represent openness to receiving a gift. The posture of one who is standing, with arms out and hands open, signifies not only openness to receive but also total vulnerability and inability to harm. Open hands are confident hands. One who wants to take something from someone, to take possession, does not open his hands but tightens them. This is the gesture of disobedience accomplished in the garden "in the beginning": "she took of its fruit and ate," says the account of Genesis (Gen 3:6). Adam's hand, outstretched

8. Christian Bobin, *Resuscitare* (Milan: Gribaudi, 2003), 9.

in a gesture of taking, is understood in Pseudo-Hippolytus's homily *In sanctum Pascha* to be an intense christological image: "[I]n place of the old tree [Christ] plants a new one; in place of the wicked hand which was formerly extended in a godless gesture, there is his own immaculate hand closed in a gesture of godliness, showing his whole life hanging [on the cross]."[9]

And so one does not grab the eucharistic bread, one doesn't take it; one receives it from someone else who puts it into our opened hands, because salvation in Christ, of whom the eucharistic bread is a sacrament, is a freely given gift of the Father. The Eastern liturgies have maintained the practice of the ancient church, in which not even the bishop or priest who presides at a liturgy takes the bread and the chalice for himself in receiving Communion but rather receives it always from another minister. No one among the faithful can confer on himself a sacrament of the church. No one baptizes herself; baptism is received, administered by someone else, a sign of the Other who baptizes. No one absolves himself of his own sins. No one imposes hands on himself for ordination. In the same way, one does not take for herself the eucharistic bread; someone else, in the name of God and on behalf of the church, gives it, putting it in your hands. This bread is the sacrament of salvation, a gift of God in Christ through the power of the Holy Spirit.

The gestures of giving and receiving are accompanied by a brief formula: "The Body of Christ," to which we respond, "Amen," the briefest but most intense word of the entire liturgy. Augustine of Hippo, in his mystagogical cate-

9. Pseudo-Hippolytus, Homily, *On the Pasch*, 50, in *Worship in the Early Church: An Anthology of Historical Sources*, trans. Lawrence J. Johnson, vol. 3 (Collegeville, MN: Liturgical Press, 2009), 240.

chesis on the Eucharist already cited, explains the meaning of the Eucharist starting from the rite of Communion and from the brief dialog, "The Body of Christ," "Amen":

> [I]f it's you that are the body of Christ and its members, it's the mystery meaning you that has been placed on the Lord's table; what you receive is the mystery that means you. It is to what you are that you reply "Amen," and by so replying you express your assent. What you hear, you see, is "The body of Christ," and you answer, "Amen." So be a member of the body of Christ, in order to make that "Amen" true.[10]

This brief text, and the entire homily from which it is taken, represents one of the most important sources of Western Eucharistic theology. It must form the eucharistic faith of every believer, and so it is always helpful to consider it further. To *become* what one receives: the body of Christ. This is why the expression "communion" indicates not only the act of receiving the Lord's body but also the purpose, the reason that we receive it: we *receive* Communion in order to *become* the communion that is the church. Every time the minister, holding up the eucharistic bread, says "The Body of Christ," he is not simply providing a definition of what he is giving. Certainly, this formula is the highest confession of the church's eucharistic faith. It confesses that that bread is the body of Christ, and the faithful respond "Amen," confirming this faith and making it their own. However, it is imperative to note that the liturgy does not have the minister say *"This is* the body of Christ," but simply *"Corpus Christi,"* "The Body of Christ." In this way the liturgy says that "The Body of Christ" is

10. St. Augustine, Sermon 272, in *Sermons*, part 3, vol. 7, trans. Edmund Hill (New Rochelle, NY: New City Press, 1993), 300.

not only an affirmative formula but also exhortative. Holding the eucharistic bread before the eyes of the faithful and saying, "The Body of Christ," is not just a doctrinal statement that what one receives is the body of the Lord; it is also a reminder to the faithful of what it means to receive in one's own hands and be nourished by the eucharistic bread: to become the body of Christ. Saying "The Body of Christ," it is as though the minister says, "Become what you receive! Be the body of Christ! Live, act, and work in the church so that the church might be what it receives: the body of Christ in history!" To this eucharistic truth, too, the believer offers her "Amen," speaks her "yes." "What you hear is 'The body of Christ,'" writes Augustine, "and you answer, 'Amen.' So be a member of the body of Christ, in order to make that 'Amen' true."

This is the authentic eucharistic faith of the church: one receives the body of Christ in order to be a member of the body of Christ. This is the purpose of the Eucharist. The liturgy teaches and transmits its eucharistic faith in this way, through this liturgical action that we've been considering. It is a very different way, but complementary to the conceptual way of theology or the didactic way of catechesis.

The Jewish philosopher Simone Weil, in her famous letter to Father Couturier in 1942, wrote with provocative and paradoxical language, "When I read the catechism of the Council of Trent, it seems as though I had nothing in common with the religion there set forth. When I read the New Testament, the mystics, the liturgy, when I watch the celebration of the mass, I feel with a sort of conviction that this faith is mine."[11] Indeed, the New Testament and the liturgy—that is, Scripture and the Tradition of which the

---

11. Simone Weil, *Letter to a Priest*, trans. A. F. Wills (London: Routledge & Keagan Paul, 1953), 9.

liturgy is the highest expression—both transmit "a kind of certainty that this is my faith."

## How the Liturgy Will Transmit the Faith Tomorrow

Half a century after the council and with challenging and decisive years ahead for the future of Christianity in the West, Christian pastors and educators must understand fully and be able to respond adequately to a need that believers today frequently express, sometimes in an ambiguous and confused way. This requires careful pastoral discernment and a clear spiritual intuition. I refer to the need to find in the liturgy a more prayerful and meditative atmosphere, the desire for a more contemplative liturgy that gives primacy to interiority and personal appropriation of what is said and done in the ritual action. To say it more simply, one could say we are talking about a more spiritual and less convivial liturgy, more contemplative and less festive, a liturgy with less words and more Word, less improvised signs and more accomplished signs.

"We are here to celebrate" is often what a community hears from its presider in greeting. But an authentic liturgical celebration is above all interior, silent, calm, and sober, because it is a feast of faith. To speak of an "interior" celebration and interiority is not to advocate a return to intimism and much less to suggest contempt for the irreplaceable bodily and sensory aspects that must necessarily mark the liturgy, it being a human action that serves human needs. Rather, to call for a more contemplative liturgy means recovering the primacy of interiority that has inadvertently been overshadowed as a result of a poorly understood and excessive emphasis on exteriorization.

To this end, in the coming years it will probably be necessary to rethink profoundly the concept of "active participation," which remains a fundamental and irreplaceable achievement of the council, a point of no return. In these recent years, based on a mistaken interpretation of "active participation," there has been perhaps too much insistence on the necessity of expressing one's feelings, of manifesting the emotions in the search for an atmosphere of encounter and celebration. Today we are remembering that the liturgy, before being an emotional encounter between people who gather, is first of all acceptance of a Word that calls together the assembly and nourishment that allows us to live what we receive. The liturgical celebration must become more truly a space of contemplation, a time of interiorization. It must be an experience of hearing the word, prayer, adoration, and real encounter with God. At the end of a Sunday eucharistic celebration, the faithful must be able to say in their hearts, "I lived a true spiritual experience that nourished me as a person and a believer." For this reason, the primary task will be to move such interiorization to the heart of the liturgy, because if the meaning of the liturgical texts and gestures are not interiorized by those who participate, these texts and gestures will never be able to nourish Christians and form their deepest identities.

Today this need of interiority is expressed above all by the serious and motivated young people who seek, in ways perhaps inarticulate but authentic, a more interior relationship with God. Most of the time, they say they do not find this in the typical liturgies that we celebrate. Suffice it here to mention a phenomenon that should now be clear to everyone in the church: the return of eucharistic adoration, above all among the young. Adoration of the Eucharist, which fosters a sacramental relationship mediated by God and instituted by the church, is an undeniable aspect of the question of a liturgy that is prayerful, meditative, silent, with few if any words necessary. Louis-Marie Chauvet reflected on this phenomenon, observing:

> The current question of eucharistic adoration, clearly resurgent in the parishes, probably must be understood as a reaction to the uncertainty of our time—a reaction in favor of a more demonstrative affirmation of the Catholic faith and in favor too of a more sensory interiorization of one's relationship with God.[12]

There is a paradox here: those young people who embrace massive and spectacular liturgies are in fact in search of a greater interiorization of their relationship with God through a more meditative and contemplative liturgy. Presbyters are called to interpret and respond to this important cue from the young. This work of discernment also calls for vigilance and a real effort of education, which means not only formation but also timely and prudent correction. In any case, our response to this demand is mandatory, or else the next generations of Christians will develop an extraliturgical spiritual life that will result in Christians without liturgy. Presbyters and educators must therefore confront and manage a new form of *devotio*—no longer *moderna* but *post-moderna*.

One somewhat worrying sign of this new *devotio* is the current exaltation—not only by anthropologists, but also by theologians and liturgists—of feelings, affections, and emotions, to which the young are by nature particularly sensitive. Human awareness and understanding necessarily include an affective and emotional component, which is essential in human experience. And yet we must be vigilant that an exaltation of the feelings and emotionalism

---

12. Louis-Marie Chauvet, "La diversité des pratiques liturgiques: quelques repères théologiques," *La Maison-Dieu* 242 (2005): 157.

does not come at the expense of rational thought, interiorization, spiritual understanding, and personal appropriation of the contents and the meaning of the liturgy. The Christian liturgy, though not solely a matter of rationality, is a *loghikè latreía*, a "worship in word" and "according to reason" (see Rom 12:1). Easy feelings and superficial affections do not, in the long run, nourish the life of the believer; we need the solid food of the word of God and the Eucharist, which have been from the beginning the only solid and substantial nourishment of the Christian. Authentic Christian liturgy is only very rarely and in extraordinary situations a source of strong emotions. One who attends the Sunday Eucharist with regularity, year after year, throughout an entire life, does not seek strong emotions but the profound consolation capable of giving strength and fortifying a faith often put to the test. She seeks the certain hope that comes from forgiveness of one's sins and from reconciliation with one's neighbors. She seeks the firm faith that comes from the word of the Gospel and, finally, she seeks the sincere love that comes from communion in the body of Christ. One who prays the Liturgy of the Hours throughout the day knows the effort of faithfulness, and she knows that the intimate consolation of the Spirit is a rare gift in the midst of frequent aridity and much exhaustion. When Bernard of Clairvaux, in his *Sermons on the Song of Songs*, describes the consolations of his encounter with the Lord, which he often calls "visits with the Word," he is quick to speak of these consolations as *"rara hora et parva mora"*—"how rare the time, and how short the stay!"[13]

13. Bernard of Clairvaux, *On the Song of Songs II*, Sermon 23.6.15, trans. Kilian Walsh (Kalamazoo, MI: Cistercian Publications, 1976), 38.

The liturgy of tomorrow then seems to call for Christians to rediscover the value of interiorization of the content of the liturgy and of a more prayerful and contemplative atmosphere. This, it seems, is one of the essential conditions—certainly not the only one but a fundamental one—that will allow the liturgy to continue to be a place of the transmission of the faith.

# Conclusion

# The Liturgy Is the Most Efficacious Action of the Church

From its very origins, the church has believed that the liturgy is its most efficacious action, because in it God, through the work of the Holy Spirit, acts in an infinitely more real and powerful way than he acts in any other activity the church carries out. The Second Vatican Council expressed this awareness in *Sacrosanctum Concilium* when it said, "Every liturgical celebration . . . is a sacred action [*actio sacra*] surpassing all others. No other action of the Church can equal its efficacy by the same title and to the same degree."[1] To believe that the liturgy is the most efficacious action of the church requires a serious journey of conversion, both personal and communal, human and pastoral.

The conditions of the *sequela Christi* that Jesus himself invites us to in the gospel are and remain not only the conditions of the life of every individual Christian but also the conditions of the ecclesial life and of all the

---

1. Second Vatican Council, *Sacrosanctum Concilium*, n. 7.

church's pastoral activity. In Luke's account of Jesus' visit to the house in Bethany—when Mary sits at the feet of Jesus to listen to his words while her sister Martha is "distracted by her many tasks" (Luke 10:40)—Mary's contemplative stance is liturgical in the most authentic and profound sense, because it is a discernment of the presence of the Lord, giving him primacy, listening to his word and to nothing else. Mary's attitude should be the model for every Christian who celebrates the liturgy. In this episode the evangelist Luke puts a clear relationship between the "many tasks" of Martha and the singular task of Mary. The *'avodà*, the "service," the only act of worship that the Lord asked of his people Israel, is *to listen to his voice*. The prophet Jeremiah preached that listening to his word, not sacrifice, was the only and true worship that God commanded Israel: "For in the day that I brought your ancestors out of the land of Egypt, I did not speak to them or command them concerning burnt offerings and sacrifices. But this command I gave them, 'Obey my voice, and I will be your God, and you shall be my people'" (Jer 7:22-23). Listening, then, is the only act of worship demanded by God from his people, the only element that God established as essential in the worship of Israel. It is the necessary condition in the celebration of praise for which God, according to the prophet Isaiah, has formed Israel as his people, "the people whom I formed for myself so that they might declare my praise" (Isa 43:21). Listening is the "one thing" needed (see. Luke 10:42) in order to adore the Lord in true worship. What Jeremiah said to Israel, Jesus said to Martha—"there is need of only one thing," adding: "Mary has chosen the better part [*optimum partem*], which will not be taken away from her" (Luke 10:42). The *optima pars* will never be kept from those who choose it for themselves.

Among the many activities of the Christian community, the *'avodà*—the service of God, the liturgy—is the "one thing" that is needed. It is the "better part" to be chosen. For different reasons in recent decades, this may have been somewhat forgotten amidst the church's activities. But listening to the word and the prayer of intercession, praise, and thanksgiving together at the breaking of the bread are the *optima pars* among the works of the church that, according to Jesus, "will not be taken away" from us.

In this, the liturgical ministry of the presbyter plays a fundamental role. The presbyter must always be aware that the sacramental actions over which he presides in the name of Christ and in the name of the church are the most efficacious actions of his ministry, and nothing else he does is equal in efficacy. To believe that the liturgy is the most efficacious action of the church means that in the liturgy, more than in any other activity, the presbyter himself is not at the center, nor are his own convictions, skills, and strategies, what he wants the liturgy to do or, better, what he wants the liturgy to be. The liturgy's own efficacy is the best antidote to its instrumentalization. At times one has the impression that some presbyters understand and live the liturgy as a mere instrument that guarantees their having a gathering of people to address every Sunday, to whom they can transmit teaching of all kinds. To reduce the liturgy to this is to fail to believe in its efficacy, to fail to believe that the word of the Lord alone (not human words) speaks to the hearts of people. It is to fail to believe that it is only the Holy Spirit, through the word and the sacraments, who generates, nourishes, and causes the growth of a Christian's life of faith—not the busyness, the innumerable, frantic, and at times anxiety-producing pastoral activities. Cardinal Godfried Danneels wrote forcefully about the origins and the purpose of the liturgy:

Often the liturgy becomes a school. We want it to do everything. Rather, it must remain a symbolic and playful activity. The true liturgy is celebrated in monasteries. There, at least, it does not serve any other purpose! It is not catechesis and the homilies are short. It is not particularly artistic, but it is beautiful in itself. In consists in the hearty welcoming of Christ through the liturgical action. The soul and the body are captured, even when the intellect has not understood everything.[2]

The church of tomorrow either will be liturgical or it will not be fully itself. It will either rediscover the primacy of the celebration of faith, or it will lose something essential. For presbyters to carry out their liturgical ministry with skill and wisdom means to work for a church that is less bureaucratic and more contemplative. It is to discern the *unum necessarium*, to choose the *optima pars* that will not be kept from us.

We must invest much human and spiritual effort in the liturgy and the sacramental life, with the certainty that the liturgy is more necessary than useful, despite the efforts and incomprehension of those who minimize and misunderstand its importance. To value liturgical space, the arts, chant, music, the sounds of an instrument, the beauty of a gesture or a fabric or the scent of incense—these must not be considered useless or unnecessary. Cristina Campo, the writer and poet, a believer and a great lover of the liturgy, has written: "The liturgy—like poetry—is gratuitous splendor, delicate waste, more necessary than useful."[3]

Indeed, the liturgy is more necessary than useful, because the liturgy has its roots in that jar of precious nard

2. Godfried Danneels, "Comment entrons-nous dans la liturgie?" *La Documentation Catholique* 2132 (1996): 173.

3. Cristina Campo, *Sotto falso nome* (Milan: Adelphi, 1998), 127.

that a woman poured on the head and the feet of Jesus as a prophecy of his death. One has the distinct impression that Jesus was fascinated by that enchanting waste on his behalf, representing nothing other than for love of him. Jesus compared that waste to the short-sighted philanthropy of Judas who, playing a role we know well, claimed the money for the poor. We know what Judas said: "Why was this perfume not sold for three hundred denarii and the money given to the poor?" (John 12:5). And we also know well Jesus' response: "You always have the poor with you, but you do not always have me" (John 12:8). Cristina Campo comments: "God is not always there and does not stay long, and when he is, we must not be distracted by other thoughts or concerns."[4]

Even God loves the gratuitous gestures, done only for love of him, like the anointing of the body of Jesus by that woman. "The house was filled with the fragrance of the perfume," says John's account (John 12:3). In that perfume of precious nard we see every Christian liturgy, because the liturgy is "gratuitous splendor, delicate waste, more necessary than useful." We must guard carefully the liturgy of the church and, by guarding it, transmit the church's faith into the future.

4. Ibid.